UNDERSTANDING AND USING

ENGLISH GRAMMAR

Third Edition

Workbook

Volume B

Betty Schrampfer Azar

Chief contributor: Rachel Spack Koch
Contributors: Susan Jamieson
          Barbara Andrews
          Jeanie Francis
          Donald A. Azar

Longman

Editorial director: *Allen Ascher*
Executive editor: *Louisa Hellegers*
Development editor: *Janet Johnston*
Director of design and production: *Rhea Banker*
Associate director of electronic publishing: *Aliza Greenblatt*
Managing editor: *Shelley Hartle*
Electronic production editor: *Rachel Baumann*
Associate art director: *Carey Davies*
Senior manufacturing manager: *Patrice Fraccio*
Production manager: *Ray Keating*
Manufacturing buyer: *Dave Dickey*
Production assistant: *Donna Stevenson*
Illustrator: *Don Martinetti*

Published by Pearson Education
10 Bank Street, White Plains, N.Y. 10606

Printed in the United States of America
10 9 8 7 6 5 4 3 2

ISBN 0-13-958760-8

CONTENTS

Chapter 14 GERUNDS AND INFINITIVES, PART 1

Chapter 15 GERUNDS AND INFINITIVES, PART 2

Chapter 16 COORDINATING CONJUNCTIONS

Chapter 20 CONDITIONAL SENTENCES AND WISHES

Appendix   SUPPLEMENTARY GRAMMAR UNITS

Special Workbook Section

PHRASAL VERBS

PRACTICE   PAGE

Preface

This ELT *Workbook* is a place for students to explore and practice English grammar on their own. It is a place where they can test and fine-tune their understandings of English structures and improve their abilities to use English meaningfully and correctly.

It is keyed to the explanatory grammar charts found in *Understanding and Using English Grammar, Third Edition,* a classroom teaching text for students of English as a second or foreign language, as well as in the accompanying *Chartbook,* a reference grammar with no exercises.

The *Workbook* is designed not only for students who desire the opportunity for independent study of English grammar, but also as a resource for teachers who need exercise material for additional classwork, homework, testing, or individualized instruction.

The answers to ALL of the practices are given in the back of the book in an *Answer Key.* The *Answer Key* is on perforated pages so that it can be detached to construct a separate booklet. If teachers desire to use the *Workbook* as a classroom teaching text, the *Answer Key* can be removed at the beginning of the term.

A note on changes from the previous edition: The *Workbook* that accompanied the previous edition of *Understanding and Using English Grammar* had both self-study (answers given) and guided study (no answers given) practices. This *Workbook* has only self-study practices. The guided study practices that involved communicative, interactive, and/or task-based activities are now in the main teaching text, and other guided study practices from the previous edition have been adapted to a self-study format in this edition. Another change is that the presentation of phrasal verbs was deleted from the main text and is now found in a special supplementary section in this *Workbook.*

Acknowledgments

The multi-talented Shelley Hartle, my associate in all work matters, and the masterful Janet Johnston, my longtime editor, are indispensable to the production of the Azar texts. I owe them great gratitude — and also thoroughly enjoy their friendship. In particular, they have expertly handled all the many editorial and production tasks demanded by this *Workbook* and its accompanying *Chartbook*.

Longtime users of my textbooks may have noted the change in publisher. My textbooks had a Prentice Hall imprint for nineteen years; that imprint is now changing to Longman due to a recent corporate acquisition. Both imprints represent quality academic publication.

I am pleased to have my work join Longman's long history of publishing excellence in the area of teaching English to speakers of other languages. My own commitment to quality publication matches well with the Longman tradition.

I wish to thank those at Prentice Hall Regents who helped make my association with that publisher one of mutual respect and enjoyment in recent years, in particular Robin Baliszewski and Mary Jane Peluso.

I also wish at this time to thank those at Pearson Education, the owners of the Longman imprint, who have eased my transition to a new publishing company. In particular I wish to thank Joanne Dresner, Allen Ascher, and Louisa Hellegers for their open, professional, and friendly management styles. I look forward to a long and rewarding relationship.

Others at Pearson Education I wish to thank are Rachel Baumann, Carey Davies, Aliza Greenblatt, and Ray Keating. Thanks are also due to Donna Stevenson, who input the entire *Workbook* on disk from a giant cut-and-paste puzzle.

Last, I wish to thank Larry Harris, my husband, for teaching me how to play. Hard work has always come easily to me, but not how to play. Now there's balance.

CHAPTER 12
Noun Clauses

◇ **PRACTICE 1. Questions and noun clauses that begin with a question word.**
(Charts 12-1 and 12-2; Appendix Charts B-1 and B-2)

Directions: Identify noun clauses and questions. Look at the <u>underlined</u> part of each sentence. If the underlined part is a question, circle **Q**. If it is a noun clause, circle **N.Cl.** Add the necessary punctuation.

1. Ⓠ N.Cl.   I couldn't hear him.   <u>What did he say</u>**?**

2. Q Ⓝ.Cl.   I couldn't hear <u>what he said</u>**.**

3. Q N.Cl.   I need some information.   <u>Where does Tom live</u>   I have to send him a letter.

4. Q N.Cl.   I need to know <u>where Tom lives</u>   I have to send him a letter.

5. Q N.Cl.   There's something I don't understand.   <u>Why did Barb cancel her vacation plans</u>

6. Q N.Cl.   I don't understand <u>why Barb canceled her vacation plans</u>

7. Q N.Cl.   I can't tell you <u>what they did</u>   You'll have to ask Jim.

8. Q N.Cl.   <u>What did they do</u>   Please tell me.

9. Q N.Cl.   Do you know that woman?   <u>Who is she</u>   She looks familiar.

10. Q N.Cl.   Do you see that woman over there?   Do you know <u>who she is</u>   She looks familiar.

11. Q N.Cl.   <u>Where did Ann go</u>   Do you know?

12. Q N.Cl.   <u>Where Ann went</u>   is a secret

◇ **PRACTICE 2. Questions and noun clauses that begin with a question word.**
(Charts 12-1 and 12-2; Appendix Charts B-1 and B-2)

Directions: If the given words are a question, insert a capital letter and a question mark. If the given words are a noun clause, write "I don't know" and a final period.

1. _____ W̶ where is he**?** _____

2. _____ I don't know where he is**.** _____

3. _____ I don't know what he did**.** _____

4. _____ W̶ what did he do**?** _____

5. _____ how old is he _____

6. _____ how old he is _____

7. _____ where did he go _____

8. _____ where he went _____

9. _____ why he said that _____

10. _____ why did he say that _____

11. _____ who he is _____

12. _____ who is he _____

13. _____ when will he arrive _____

14. _____ when he will arrive _____

15. _____ who is he talking to _____

16. _____ which one he bought _____

◇ **PRACTICE 3. Questions and noun clauses that begin with a question word.**
   (Charts 12-1 and 12-2; Appendix Charts B-1 and B-2)

Directions: Make a question from the given sentence. The words in parentheses should be the answer to the question you make. Use a question word (**who, what, how,** etc.). Then change the question to a noun clause.

1. That man is *(Mr. Robertson).*

   QUESTION: ___Who is that man?_____

   NOUN CLAUSE: I want to know ___who that man is._____

2. George lives *(in Los Angeles).*

   QUESTION: _____

   NOUN CLAUSE: I want to know _____

3. Ann bought *(a new dictionary).*

   QUESTION: _____

   NOUN CLAUSE: Do you know _____

4. It is *(350 miles)* to Denver from here.

   QUESTION: _____

   NOUN CLAUSE: I need to know _____

5. Jack was late to class *(because he missed the bus).*

   QUESTION: _____

   NOUN CLAUSE: The teacher wants to know _____

Noun Clauses **117**

6. That is *(Ann's)* pen.

QUESTION: _____

NOUN CLAUSE: Tom wants to know _____

7. Alex saw *(Ms. Frost)* at the meeting.

QUESTION: _____

NOUN CLAUSE: I don't know _____

8. *(Jack)* saw Ms. Frost at the meeting.

QUESTION: _____

NOUN CLAUSE: I don't know _____

9. Alice likes *(this)* book best, *(not that one)*.

QUESTION: _____

NOUN CLAUSE: I want to know _____

10. The plane is supposed to land *(at 7:14 P.M.)*.

QUESTION: _____

NOUN CLAUSE: Could you tell me _____

◇ **PRACTICE 4. Questions and noun clauses that begin with a question word.**
   (Charts 12-1 and 12-2; Appendix Charts B-1 and B-2)

Directions: Make questions and noun clauses.

Example:
SPEAKER A: Make a question from each given sentence. The words in parentheses should be the answer to your question.
SPEAKER B: Keep your book closed. Change Speaker A's question into a noun clause. Begin your sentence with "(Name of Speaker A) wants to know . . . ."

1. Fred* lives *(in an apartment)*.
   Speaker A: Where does Fred live?
   Speaker B: (Yoko) wants to know where Fred lives.

2. It's *(ten o'clock)*.
   Speaker A: What time is it?
   Speaker B: (Roberto) wants to know what time it is.

3. Tom wants *(a watch)* for his birthday.

4. Jane gets to school *(by bus)*.

_____

*To Student A: Use the name of a class member instead of the name in the exercise if you wish.
 For example: *Where does Ali live?* (instead of *Where does Fred live?*)

5. Vacation starts *(on June 3rd)*.

6. Sue left class early *(because she didn't feel well)*.

7. The movie is going to last *(two hours and ten minutes)*.

8. Mary called *(Jim)*.

9. *(Mary)* called Jim.

10. Alice talked to the teacher about *(the test)*.

11. Alice talked to *(the teacher)* about the test.

12. *(Alice)* talked to the teacher about the test.

13. Sue's plane will arrive *(at 8:05)*.

14. *(Two)* students will be absent from class tomorrow.

15. There are *(over 10,000)* lakes in Minnesota.

16. It's *(twenty-five miles)* to Springfield from here.

17. Jane *(studied)* last night.

18. We're supposed to buy *(this)* book, *(not that book)*.

19. Ann likes *(chocolate)* ice cream the best.

20. A robin's egg is *(turquoise blue)*.

21. That woman is *(Mrs. Anderson)*.

22. *(Mr. Anderson)* is talking on the telephone.

23. That's *(Sam's)* notebook.

24. *(Jessica's)* car was stolen.

◇ **PRACTICE 5. Questions and noun clauses that begin with a question word.
    (Charts 12-1 and 12-2; Appendix Charts B-1 and B-2)**

Directions: Use the words in parentheses to complete the sentences. Use any appropriate verb tense. Some of the completions contain noun clauses and some contain questions.

1. A: John is searching every drawer. Do you know what ___he's looking for___ ?
   (he, look for)

   B: I have no idea. Why don't I just ask him? John? What ___are you looking for___ ?
   (you, look for)

2. A: I heard that Sam changed his mind about going on the picnic. Why _____ _____ to stay home? Is something wrong? *(he, decide)*

   B: I don't know. Maybe Jane can tell us why _____ not to come with us. Let's ask her. I hope he's okay. *(he, decide)*

3. A: Whose book _____? *(this, be)*

   B: It's not mine. I don't know whose _____. *(it, be)*

4. A: Did Jack get enough food when he went to the market? How much fish _____ _____? It takes a lot of fish to feed 12 people. *(he, buy)*

   B: Just relax. I don't know exactly how much fish _____, but I'm sure there'll be enough for dinner for all of us. *(he, buy)*

5. A: I need a math tutor. Do you know who _____? *(John's tutor, be)*

   B: No. Let me ask Phil. Excuse me, Phil? Who _____? Do you know? *(John's tutor, be)*

6. A: Lucy, why _____ for the exam? You could have done much better if you'd been prepared. *(you, study, not)*

   B: Well, Professor Morris, why _____ for the exam is a long story. I intended to, but . . . . *(I, study, not)*

◇ **PRACTICE 6. Changing yes/no and information questions to noun clauses.
   (Charts 12-2 and 12-3)**

Directions: Complete each sentence by changing the question in parentheses to a noun clause.

1. *(Will it rain?)* I wonder __if/whether it will rain__.

2. *(When will it rain?)* I wonder __when it will rain__.

3. *(Is Sam at home?)*

   I don't know _____ at home.

4. *(Where is Sam?)*

   I don't know _____.

5. *(Did Jane call?)*

   Ask Tom _____.

6. *(What time did she call?)*

   Ask Tom _____.

7. *(Why is the earth called "the water planet"?)*

   Do you know _____ "the water planet"?

8. *(How far is it from New York City to Jakarta?)*

   I wonder _____ from New York to Jakarta.

9. *(Has Susan ever been in Portugal?)*

   I wonder _____ in Portugal.

10. *(Does she speak Portuguese?)*

    I wonder _____ Portuguese.

11. *(Who did Ann play tennis with?)*

    I wonder _____ tennis with.

12. *(Who won the tennis match?)*

    I wonder _____ the tennis match.

13. *(Did Ann win?)*

    I wonder _____ .

14. *(Do all creatures, including fish and insects, feel pain in the same way as humans do?)*

    I wonder _____

    pain in the same way as humans do.

15. *(Can birds communicate with each other?)*

    Do you know _____ with each other?

16. *(How do birds communicate with each other?)*

    Have you ever studied _____ with each other?

17. *(Where is the nearest post office?)*

    Do you know _____ ?

18. *(Is there a post office near here?)*

    Do you know _____ near here?

◇ **PRACTICE 7. Question words and *whether* followed by infinitives. (Chart 12-4)**
Directions: Using the idea in the question in parentheses, complete each sentence with a question word or ***whether*** followed by an infinitive.

1. *(Where should I buy the meat for the lamb stew?)*
I don't know ___where to buy___ the meat for the lamb stew.

2. *(Should I stay home or go to the movie?)*
Tom can't decide ___whether to stay___ home or ___go___ to the movie.

3. *(How can I fix the toaster?)*
Jack doesn't know ___how to fix___ the toaster.

4. *(Should I look for another job?)*
Jason is wondering ___whether (or not) to look___ for another job.

5. *(Where can I get a map of the city?)*
Ann wants to know _____ a map of the city.

6. *(Should I go to the meeting?)*
Al is trying to decide _____ to the meeting.

7. *(What time should I pick you up?)*
I need to know _____ you up.

8. *(Who should I talk to about this problem?)*
I don't know _____ to about this problem.

9. *(Should I take a nap or do my homework?)*
I can't decide _____ a nap or _____ my homework.

10. *(How can I solve this problem for you?)*
My adviser can't figure out _____ this problem for me.

11. *(Where should I tell them to meet us?)*
I'm not sure _____ them to meet us.

12. *(How long am I supposed to cook this meat?)*
I can't remember _____ this meat.

13. *(What should I wear to the ceremony?)*
I can't decide _____ to the ceremony.

14. *(How much coffee should I make for the meeting?)*
You'll have to tell me _____ for the meeting.

15. *(Which essay should I use for the contest?)*
Susan can't decide _____ for the contest.

16. *(Should I take a year off from work and travel around the world? Or should I keep working and save my money?)*
Alice can't decide _____ a year off from work and _____

around the world, or _____ working and _____ her money.

◇ **PRACTICE 8. *That*-clauses. (Chart 12-5)**

Directions: Combine each pair of sentences into one that contains a noun clause. Begin the new sentence with ***That*** or ***It***.

Examples: The weather is not going to improve. That is apparent.
→ *It is apparent that the weather is not going to improve.* OR
That the weather is not going to improve is apparent.

Pollution diminishes the quality of our lives. That is hard to deny.
→ *That pollution diminishes the quality of our lives is hard to deny.* OR
It is hard to deny that pollution diminishes the quality of our lives.

1. No one stopped to help Sam when he had car trouble. That is surprising.

2. People in modern cities are distrustful of each other. That is unfortunate.

3. People in my village always help each other. That is still true.

4. People need each other and need to help each other. That is undeniably true.

5. People have a moral duty to help others in need. That seems obvious to me.

6. People today are afraid to help strangers. That is a pity.

7. People in cities live in densely populated areas but don't know their neighbors. That seems strange to me.

◇ **PRACTICE 9. Using *the fact that*. (Chart 12-5)**

Directions: Combine each pair of sentences into one sentence by using ***the fact that***.

1. I studied for three months for the examination. Regardless of that, I barely passed.
→ *Regardless of **the fact that** I studied for three months for the examination, I barely passed.*

2. Jim lost our tickets to the concert. There's nothing we can do about that.

3. We are going to miss one of the best concerts of the year because of Jim's carelessness. That makes me a little angry.

4. We can't go to the concert. In view of that, let's plan to go to a movie.

5. I couldn't speak a word of Italian and understood very little. Except for that, I had a wonderful time visiting my Italian cousins in Rome.

6. Many people living in Miami speak only Spanish. When I first visited Florida, I was surprised by that.

7. Bobby broke my grandmother's antique flower vase. That isn't important.

8. He lied about it. That is what bothers me.

9. Prof. Brown, who had had almost no teaching experience, was hired to teach the advanced physics courses. At first, some of us objected to that, but she has proven herself to be one of the best.

10. That automobile has the best safety record of any car manufactured this year. I am impressed by that and would definitely recommend that you buy that make.

◇ **PRACTICE 10. Quoted speech. (Chart 12-6)**
Directions: Add the necessary punctuation and capitalization to these sentences. Do not change the word order or add or delete any words.

1. The athlete said where is my uniform
   → *The athlete said, "Where is my uniform?"*

2. I can't remember Margaret said where I put my purse

3. Sandy asked her sister how can I help you get through this difficulty

4. I'll answer your question later he whispered I'm trying to hear what the speaker is saying

5. As the students entered the room, the teacher said please take your seats quickly

6. Why did I ever take this job Barry wondered aloud

7. After crashing into me and knocking all of my packages to the ground, the man stopped abruptly, turned to me and said softly excuse me

8. Do we want four more years of corruption and debt the candidate shouted into the microphone no the crowd screamed

9. The woman behind the fast-food counter shouted who's next

   I am three people replied at the same time

   Which one of you is really next she asked impatiently

   I was here first said a young woman elbowing here way up to the counter I want a hamburger

   You were not hollered an older man standing next to her I was here before you were give me a chicken sandwich and a cup of coffee

   Wait a minute I was in line first said a young man give me a cheeseburger and a chocolate shake

   The woman behind the restaurant counter spotted a little boy politely waiting his turn she turned to him and said hi, Sonny what can I get for you

◇ PRACTICE 11. Reported speech. (Chart 12-7)

Directions: Change the sentences by changing quoted to reported speech. Use formal sequence of tenses.

1. Tom said, "I am busy." → Tom said that he __was__ busy.

2. Tom said, "I need some help." → Tom said that he _____ some help.

3. Tom said, "I am having a good time." → Tom said that he _____ a good time.

4. Tom said, "I have finished my work." → Tom said that he _____ his work.

5. Tom said, "I finished it an hour ago." → Tom said that he _____ it an hour ago.

6. Tom said, "I will arrive at noon." → Tom said that he _____ at noon.

7. Tom said, "I am going to be there at noon." → Tom said that he _____ there at noon.

8. Tom said, "I can solve that problem." → Tom said that he _____ that problem.

9. Tom said, "I may come early." → Tom said that he _____ early.

10. Tom said, "I might come early." → Tom said that he _____ early.

11. Tom said, "I must leave at eight." → Tom said that he _____ at eight.

12. Tom said, "I have to leave at eight." → Tom said that he _____ at eight.

13. Tom said, "I should go to the library." → Tom said that he _____ to the library.

14. Tom said, "I ought to go to the library." → Tom said that he _____ to the library.

15. Tom said, "Stay here." → Tom told me _____ here.

16. Tom said, "Don't move." → Tom told me _____ .

17. Tom said, "Are you comfortable?" → Tom asked me if I _____ comfortable.

18. Tom said, "When did you arrive?" → Tom asked me when I _____ .

◇ PRACTICE 12. Reported speech. (Chart 12-7)

Directions: Complete the sentences by changing the quoted speech to reported speech. Use formal sequence of tenses as appropriate. (Pay attention to whether the reporting verb is past or present.)

1. *I asked Martha, "Are you planning to enter law school?"*

   I asked Martha ___if/whether she was planning___ to enter law school.

2. *Ed just asked me, "What time does the movie begin?"*

   Ed wants to know ___what time the movie begins___ .

3. *Fred asked, "Can we still get tickets for the concert?"*

   Fred asked ___if/whether we could still get___ tickets for the concert.

4. *Thomas said to us, "How can I help you?"*

   Thomas wants to know _____how he can help_____ us.

5. *Eva asked, "Can you help me, John?"*

   Eva asked John _____ her.

6. *Charles said, "When will the final decision be made?"*

   Charles wanted to know _____ .

7. *Frank asked Elizabeth, "Where have you been all afternoon?"*

   Frank asked Elizabeth _____ all afternoon.

8. *Bill just said, "What is Kim's native language?"*

   Bill wants to know _____ .

9. *Yesterday Ron said to Bob, "What's the problem?"*

   Ron asked Bob _____ .

10. *I asked myself, "Am I doing the right thing?"*

    I wondered _____ the right thing.

11. *All of the farmers are asking, "When is this terrible drought going to end?"*

    All of the farmers are wondering _____ to end.

12. *George asked me, "What time do I have to be at the laboratory in the morning?"*

    George asked me _____ to be at the laboratory in the morning.

13. *Beth asked, "Who should I give this message to?"*

    Beth asked me _____ .

14. *Our tour guide said, "We'll be leaving around 7:00 in the morning."*

    Our tour guide told us _____ around 7:00 in the morning.

15. *Nancy asked, "Why didn't you call me?"*

    Nancy wanted to know _____ her.

◇ **PRACTICE 13. Reported speech. (Chart 12-7)**

   Directions: Complete the sentences using the information in the dialogue. Use past verb forms in the noun clauses if appropriate and possible.

1. *Joanne asked me, "Do you know Dave Clark?"*
   "Yes," I replied. "I've known him for many years. Why do you want to know?"

   Joanne asked me if I __knew__ Dave Clark. I replied that I __had known__ him

   for many years and asked her why she __wanted__ to know.

2. *I asked Mary, "Why do you still smoke?"*
   Mary replied, "I've tried to quit many times, but I just don't seem to be able to."

   When I asked Mary why she _____ , she replied that she _____

   _____ to quit many times, but she just _____ to be able to.

3. *The teacher asked, "Bobby, what is the capital of Australia?"*
   Bobby replied, "I'm not sure, but I think it's Sydney."

   Yesterday in class, Bobby's teacher asked him _____. He

   answered that he _____ sure, but that he _____

   Sydney.

4. *The children inquired of their father, "Will we be able to visit the Air and Space Museum and the*
   Natural History Museum, too?"
   Their father said, "We will if we leave the hotel before 10 o'clock tomorrow morning."

   The children asked their father whether they _____ able to visit the

   Air and Space Museum and the Natural History Museum, too. He told them they

   _____ if they _____ the hotel before 10 o'clock the next morning.

5. *I told Jenny, "It's pouring outside. You'd better take an umbrella."*
   Jenny said, "It'll stop soon. I don't need one."

   I told Jenny that it _____ outside and that she _____ an

   umbrella. However, Jenny said she thought the rain _____ soon and that she

   _____ one.

6. *"Where are you going, Ann?" I asked.*
   "I'm on my way to the market," she replied. "Do you want to come with me?"
   "I'd like to, but I have to stay home. I have a lot of work to do."
   "Okay," Ann said. "Is there anything I can pick up for you at the market?"
   "How about a few bananas? And some apples if they're fresh?"
   "Sure. I'd be happy to."

   When I asked Ann where she _____, she said she _____ on

   her way to the market and _____ me to come with her. I said I

   _____ to, but that I _____ to stay home because I _____ a lot of

   work to do. Ann kindly asked me if there _____ anything she _____

   pick up for me at the market. I asked her to pick up a few bananas and some apples if they

   _____ fresh. She said she'd be happy to.

7. *"Where are you from?" asked the passenger sitting next to me on the plane.*
   "Chicago," I said.
   "That's nice. I'm from Mapleton. It's a small town in northern Michigan. Have you heard of it?"
   "Oh yes, I have," I said. "Michigan is a beautiful state. I've been there on vacation many times."
   "Were you in Michigan on vacation this year?"
   "No. I went far away from home this year. I went to India," I replied.
   "Oh, that's nice. Is it a long drive from Chicago to India?" she asked me. My mouth fell open.
   I didn't know how to respond. Some people certainly need to study geography.

The passenger sitting next to me on the plane _____ me where I _____ from. I _____ her I _____ from Chicago. She _____ that she _____ from Mapleton, a small town in northern Michigan. She wondered if I _____ _____ of it, and I told her that I _____ . I went on to say that I thought Michigan _____ a beautiful state and explained that I _____ there on vacation many times. She _____ me if I _____ in Michigan on vacation this year. I replied that I _____ and _____ her that I _____ far away, to India. Then she asked me if it _____ a long drive from Chicago to India! My mouth fell open. I didn't know how to respond. Some people certainly need to study geography.

◇ **PRACTICE 14. Using the subjunctive. (Chart 12-8)**
   Directions: Complete the sentences, using the idea of the words in parentheses.

1. *(You should organize a camping trip.)*
   The girls proposed that their scout leader __organize__ a camping trip.

2. *(Ms. Hanson thinks that the director should divide our class into two sections.)*
   Ms. Hanson recommended that our class __be divided__ into two sections.

3. *(You must call home every week.)*
   Dan's parents insisted that he _____ home every week.

4. *(Someone must tell her the truth about her illness.)*
   It is essential that she _____ the truth about her illness.

5. *(Open your suitcases for inspection.)*
   The customs official demanded that all passengers _____ their suitcases.

6. *(Ann, you should take some art courses.)*
   The counselor recommended that Ann _____ some art courses.

7. *(All parts of the motor must work correctly.)*
   It is vital that all parts of the motor _____ in proper working order.

8. *(Please mail all packages at the central office.)*
   The director requests that all packages _____ at the central office.

9. *(Soldiers must obey their officers.)*
   It is imperative that soldiers _____ their officers.

10. *(We must remember to give the babysitter certain phone numbers to call in case of emergency.)*
    It is important that the babysitter _____ phone numbers to call in case of emergency.

◇ **PRACTICE 15. Using -ever words. (Chart 12-9)**
   Directions: Complete these sentences by using *-ever* words.

   1. As vice-president of international sales, Robert has complete control over his travel schedule.
      He can travel ___whenever___ he wants.

   2. Robert is free to decide which countries he will visit during his overseas trips. He can travel
      ___wherever___ he wants.

   3. The English professor told us that we could write our papers on _____
      subject we wanted as long as it related to the topics we discussed in class this semester.

   4. There are only two appointment time slots remaining. You may select _____
      one you prefer.

   5. To Ellen, the end justifies the means. She will do _____ she has to do
      in order to accomplish her objective.

   6. Linda is very amiable and gregarious. She makes friends with _____
      she meets.

   7. It doesn't matter which class you take to fulfill this requirement. Just take _____
      one fits best into your schedule.

   8. _____ is the last to leave the room should turn off the lights and lock
      the door.

   9. I know that Norman will succeed. He'll do _____ is required to succeed.

   10. My wife and I are going to ride our bicycles across the country. We will ride for six to seven
       hours every day, then stop _____ we happen to be at the end of the day.

◇ PRACTICE 16. TEST A: Noun clauses. (Chapter 12)

Directions: In each sentence, select the ONE correct answer.

Example: He asked me where ___B___ .
   A. did I live   B. I lived   C. do you live   D. that I lived

1. I talked to Bob two weeks ago. I thought he wanted to know about my cat, but I misunderstood him. He asked me where _____, not my cat.
   A. is my hat   B. my hat was   C. my hat is   D. was my hat

2. "The people in the apartment upstairs must have a lot of children."
   "I don't know how many _____, but it sounds like they have a dozen."
   A. children do they have   C. children they have
   B. do they have children   D. they have children

3. Do you know _____? I myself have no idea.
   A. how many years the earth is   C. how long is the earth
   B. how old the earth is   D. how much time has been the earth

4. "There's too much noise in this room. I can't understand what _____."
   A. is the professor saying   C. that the professor is saying
   B. is saying the professor   D. the professor is saying

5. When I was little, my father gave me some advice. He said _____ talk to strangers.
   A. I shouldn't   B. that shouldn't   C. don't   D. that I don't

6. "I didn't expect Ann's husband to be here at the opera with her."
   "I'm surprised, too. Ann must have insisted that _____ with her."
   A. he come   B. he comes   C. he came   D. he had come

7. "Ms. Wright, can you give me a little extra help typing some letters today?"
   "Sorry, I can't. The boss has an urgent report for me to write. She demanded that it _____ on her desk by 5 P.M. today."
   A. was   B. will be   C. is   D. be

8. "Did you tell Carol where _____ us this evening?"
   "Yes, I did. I can't understand why she is late."
   A. should she meet   C. she meets
   B. she to meet   D. to meet

9. A fortune-teller predicted _____ inherit a lot of money before the end of the year.
   A. that I would   B. that I   C. what I will   D. what I

10. "Bill Frazer seems like a good person for the job, but we don't know why he left his last job."
    "I know why. He told me _____ a serious policy disagreement with his boss last January."
    A. if he'd had   B. he'd had   C. what he'd had   D. that what he had

11. "Is it true that you fell asleep in class yesterday and began to snore?"
    "Unfortunately, yes. _____ is unbelievable! I'm very embarrassed."
    A. That I could do such a thing it   C. I could do such a thing it
    B. That I could do such a thing   D. I could do such a thing

12. "Officer, can you tell me how to get to Springfield?"
    "Sure. What part of Springfield _____ to go to?"
    A. do you want   B. you want   C. that you want   D. where you want

13. "Is it true _____ the law says there is no smoking in restaurants in this city?"
    A. that what   B. what   C. if   D. that

14. _____ prompt is important to our boss.
    A. A person is   C. If a person is
    B. Is a person   D. Whether or not a person is

15. A scientific observer of wildlife must note every detail of how _____ in their environment:
    their eating and sleeping habits, their social relationships, and their methods of self-
    protection.
    A. do animals live   B. live animals   C. do live animals   D. animals live

16. The mystery movie was clever and suspenseful. The audience couldn't guess _____
    committed the murder until the surprise ending.
    A. who he   B. who had   C. that who   D. that

17. How do you like your new school? Tell me _____ .
    A. who in your class is   C. who is in your class
    B. who your class is in   D. your class who is in it

18. "What do you recommend _____ about this tax problem?"
    "I strongly suggest that we consult an expert as soon as possible."
    A. do we do   B. we will do   C. we do   D. should we do

19. The college does not grant degrees simply to _____ pays the cost of tuition; the student
    must satisfy the academic requirements.
    A. whoever   B. who   C. whomever   D. whoever that

20. "What are you going to buy in this store?"
    "Nothing. _____ want is much too expensive."
    A. That I   B. What I   C. That what I   D. What do I

◇ **PRACTICE 17. TEST B: Noun clauses. (Chapter 12)**

Directions: In each sentence, select the ONE correct answer.

Example: He asked me where ___B___ .
    A. did I live   B. I lived   C. do you live   D. that I lived

1. "Does anybody know _____ on the ground?"
   "Your guess is as good as mine."
       A. how long this plane will be   C. how long will this plane be
       B. how long will be this plane   D. that how long this plane will be

2. "This restaurant is very expensive!"
   "It is, but order _____ want. Your birthday is a very special occasion."
       A. what is it you   C. whatever you
       B. what do you   D. whatever you do

3. Why did Beth ask you _____ a bicycle?
       A. that if you had   B. do you have   C. that you had   D. if you had

4. "What did your grammar teacher want to talk to you about?"
   "I did badly on the last test. She _____ studied for it."
       A. said why hadn't I   C. said why I hadn't
       B. asked why hadn't I   D. asked why I hadn't

5. "Why are you staring out the window? What _____ about?"
   "Nothing."
       A. you are thinking   C. are you thinking
       B. you think   D. do you are thinking

6. "I can't decide what color I want for my bedroom. What do you think?"
   "You should choose _____ color you want. You're the one who will have to live with it."
       A. whichever that   B. whatever   C. however   D. that what

7. "Did you remember to tell Marge _____ she should bring to the meeting tomorrow?"
   "Oh, my gosh! I completely forgot! I'm sorry."
       A. that   B. what   C. if   D. that what

8. "My aunt has been feeling bad since Uncle George died. Is it because she's depressed?"
   "I think so. _____ can cause debilitating physical symptoms is a medical fact."
       A. Depression   C. That depression
       B. That depression it   D. It is that depression

9. There was an earthquake on the coast yesterday. Fortunately, there was no loss of life.
   However, because of the danger of collapsing sea walls, it was essential that the area _____
   evacuated quickly.
       A. to be   B. will be   C. be   D. is

10. _____ saying was so important that I asked everyone to stop talking and listen.
       A. What the woman was   C. That the woman was
       B. The woman was   D. What was the woman

11. "This cake is terrible. What happened?"
    "It's my grandmother's recipe, but she forgot to tell me how long _____ it."
    A. did I bake   B. should I bake   C. do I bake   D. to bake

12. "Let's go to to Riverton this weekend."
    "Sounds like fun. _____ from here?"
    A. How far is   B. How far it is   C. It how far is   D. How far is it

13. "Somebody forgot this hat. I wonder _____."
    A. whose is this hat   C. whose hat is
    B. whose hat this is   D. is this whose hat

14. Edward's interview was very intense. The interviewer wanted to know many facts about his
    personal life, and even asked him _____ had ever used any illegal drugs of any kind.
    A. that if he   B. that he   C. if or not he   D. whether or not he

15. It is hoped that all present-day communicable diseases will be conquered. However,
    _____ about certain diseases is still not sufficient to prevent them from spreading easily
    among the population.
    A. what we know   C. what we know that
    B. what do we know   D. that we know what

16. "Why didn't Henry attend the meeting this morning?"
    "He's been very sick. His doctor insisted that he _____ in bed this week."
    A. will stay   B. stayed   C. stays   D. stay

17. Nobody yet knew what _____ to cause the dam to burst, but the residents of the area
    organized quickly to protect life and property against the rising floods.
    A. happens   B. had happened   C. happen   D. did it happen

18. Did the teacher explain how _____ this problem?"
    A. do we solve   B. can we solve   C. to solve   D. solve

19. _____ the National Weather Bureau predicted severe storms did not deter the fishing boats
    from going out into the open seas.
    A. The fact that   B. That fact is that   C. Is fact that   D. The fact is that

20. Tom walked into the huge hall to register for classes. At first, he simply looked around and
    wondered what _____ supposed to do.
    A. was he   B. am I   C. he was   D. I am

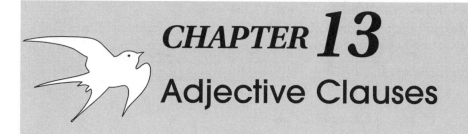

CHAPTER 13
Adjective Clauses

◇ **PRACTICE 1. Basic patterns of adjective clauses. (Charts 13-1 → 13-4)**
Directions: <u>Underline</u> the adjective clauses in these sentences.

1. a. The paintings <u>that are marked with a small red dot</u> have already been sold.
   b. The paintings <u>which are marked with a small red dot</u> have already been sold.

2. a. The secretary who sits at the first desk on the right can give you the information.
   b. The secretary that sits at the first desk on the right can give you the information.

3. a. The shoes that I bought were made in Italy.
   b. The shoes which I bought were made in Italy.
   c. The shoes I bought were made in Italy.

4. a. I wrote a letter to the woman that I met at the meeting.
   b. I wrote a letter to the woman who(m) I met at the meeting.
   c. I wrote a letter to the woman I met at the meeting.

5. a. The speech we listened to last night was informative.
   b. The speech that we listened to last night was informative.
   c. The speech which we listened to last night was informative.
   d. The speech to which we listened last night was informative.

6. a. Dr. Jones is the professor I told you about.
   b. Dr. Jones is the professor who(m) I told you about.
   c. Dr. Jones is the professor that I told you about.
   d. Dr. Jones is the professor about whom I told you.

7. The student whose parents you just met is in one of my classes.

8. The pianist who played at the concert last night is internationally famous.

9. Some of the people a waiter has to serve at a restaurant are rude.

10. The restaurant Bob recommended was too expensive.

11. Thomas Raven is a physicist whose book on time and space has been translated into a dozen languages.

12. The woman who lives next door to us is a weathercaster on a local TV station.

◇ **PRACTICE 2. Basic patterns of adjective clauses. (Charts 13-1 → 13-4)**

Directions: In the spaces, write all the pronouns possible to complete each sentence. Write Ø if the sentence is correct without adding a pronoun.

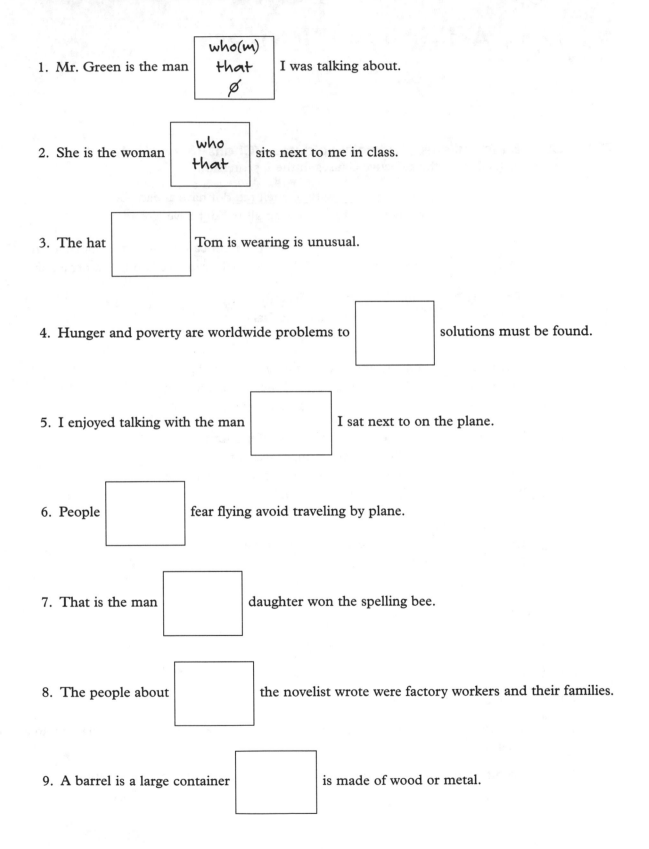

1. Mr. Green is the man | who(m) / that / ø | I was talking about.

2. She is the woman | who / that | sits next to me in class.

3. The hat | | Tom is wearing is unusual.

4. Hunger and poverty are worldwide problems to | | solutions must be found.

5. I enjoyed talking with the man | | I sat next to on the plane.

6. People | | fear flying avoid traveling by plane.

7. That is the man | | daughter won the spelling bee.

8. The people about | | the novelist wrote were factory workers and their families.

9. A barrel is a large container | | is made of wood or metal.

◇ **PRACTICE 3. Basic patterns of adjective clauses. (Charts 13-1 → 13-4)**
Directions: Write all the pronouns possible to complete each sentence. Write Ø if the sentence is correct without adding a pronoun.

PART I. Using subject pronouns in adjective clauses.

1. The bat is the only mammal [which / that] can fly.

2. People [   ] don't get enough sleep may become short-tempered and irritable.

3. The cold weather [   ] swept in from the north damaged the fruit crop.

4. Alex bought a bicycle [   ] is specially designed for long-distance racing.

5. I read about a woman [   ] makes old-fashioned clocks for a living.

PART II. Using object pronouns in adjective clauses.

6. We used the map [which / that / Ø] my sister drew for us.

7. The teacher [   ] I like the most is Mrs. Grange.

8. Louise, tell us about the movie [   ] you saw last night.

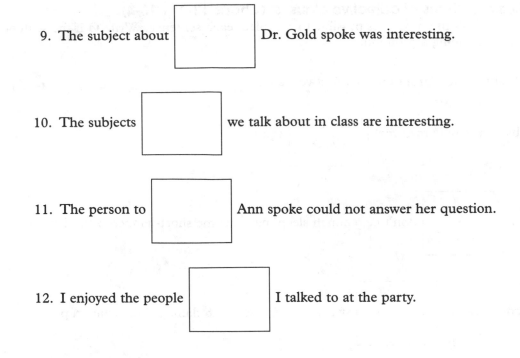

9. The subject about ☐ Dr. Gold spoke was interesting.

10. The subjects ☐ we talk about in class are interesting.

11. The person to ☐ Ann spoke could not answer her question.

12. I enjoyed the people ☐ I talked to at the party.

◇ **PRACTICE 4. Adjective clause patterns. (Charts 13-1 → 13-4)**
   Directions: Combine the sentences, using all possible forms. Use (b) as an adjective clause.

1. (a) Louis knows the woman.   (b) The woman is meeting us at the airport.
   → *Louis knows the woman* {*who* / *that*} *is meeting us at the airport.*

2. (a) The chair is an antique.   (b) Sally inherited it from her grandmother.

3. (a) The bench was wet.   (b) I sat on it.

4. (a) The man finished the job in four days.   (b) I hired him to paint my house.

5. (a) I miss seeing the old woman.   (b) She used to sell flowers on that street corner.

6. (a) The architect is brilliant.   (b) Mario works with him.

7. (a) Mary tutors students.   (b) They need extra help in geometry.

8. (a) I took a picture of the rainbow.   (b) It appeared in the sky after the shower.

◇ **PRACTICE 5. Adjective clauses: using *whose*. (Chart 13-6)**
   Directions: Combine the sentences, using *whose* in an adjective clause.

1. (a) Do you know the man?   (b) His car is parked over there.
   → *Do you know the man whose car is parked over there?*

2. (a) I know a woman.   (b) Her name is May Day.

3. (a) The people were very hospitable.   (b) We visited their home.

4. (a) The school principal walked down the hallway to find the boy.   (b) His parents had been injured in an automobile accident.

5. (a) Mrs. Lake is the teacher.   (b) I enjoy her class the most.

6. (a) Any company is stifling the creativity of its workforce.   (b) Their employees are in constant fear of losing their jobs.

◇ **PRACTICE 6. Adjective clauses: using *where* and *when*. (Charts 13-7 and 13-8)**

Directions: Begin your response with "That is . . . ." Use *where* or *when* in an adjective clause.

Example: You were born in *that* city.
Response: That is *the* city **where** I was born.

1. We have class in that room.
2. We ate dinner at that restaurant.
3. Anna works in that building
4. I was born in that year.
5. You eat lunch at that cafeteria.
6. The monsoons arrive in that month.
7. Alex lives on that street.
8. You spent your vacation on that island.
9. You went swimming in that lake.
10. You grew up in that town.
11. The space flight to Mars is scheduled to leave on that day.
12. The earthquake occurred in that country.
13. The examination will be given in that room.
14. You lived in that city until you were ten years old.
15. You felt the happiest at that time.

◇ **PRACTICE 7. Adjective clauses. (Charts 13-1 → 13-4)**

Directions: Choose the correct answer or answers.

1. Yoko told me about students __A, D__ have taken the entrance exam 13 times.
   A. who   B. whom   C. which   D. that

2. The secretary __B, C, D__ I talked to didn't know where the meeting was.
   A. which   B. whom   C. that   D. Ø

3. You need to talk to a person _____ you can trust. You will feel better if you do.
   A. whose   B. which   C. whom   D. Ø

4. Bob is the kind of person to _____ one can talk about anything.
   A. who   B. whom   C. that   D. him

5. He is a person _____ friends trust him.
   A. who   B. his   C. that   D. whose

6. I'm looking for an electric can opener _____ also can sharpen knives.
   A. who   B. which   C. that   D. Ø

7. People _____ live in glass houses shouldn't throw stones.*
   A. who   B. whom   C. which   D. Ø

8. The problems _____ Tony has seem insurmountable.
   A. what   B. he   C. that   D. Ø

---

*This is an idiom that means people shouldn't criticize others for faults they themselves have. For example, a lazy person shouldn't criticize another person for being lazy.

9. The man _____ I introduced you to last night may be the next president of the university.
   A. which   B. whom   C. that   D. Ø

10. Cathy is trustworthy. She's a person upon _____ you can always depend.
    A. who   B. whom   C. that   D. Ø

11. Your career should focus on a field in _____ you are genuinely interested.
    A. which   B. what   C. that   D. Ø

12. People _____ outlook on life is optimistic are usually happy people.
    A. whose   B. whom   C. that   D. which

◇ **PRACTICE 8. Adjective clauses: subject–verb agreement.**
           (Charts 13-1 and 13-2; Chapter 6)
   Directions: Choose the correct verb in *italics.*

   1. There are three students in my class who   *speaks,* (speak)   French.

   2. There is one student in my class who   *speaks, speak*   Greek.

   3. The patients who   *is, are*   treated at City Hospital   *doesn't, don't*   need to have private physicians.

   4. The courses this school   *offers, offer*   *is, are*   listed in the catalog.

   5. A pedometer is an instrument that   *measures, measure*   the distance a person *walks, walk.*

   6. People who   *suffers, suffer*   from extreme shyness can sometimes overcome their problem by taking a public speaking class.

   7. In the months that   *has, have*   passed since the accident, Robert has regained the use of his legs.

   8. Malnutrition and illiteracy are among the problems in the world that   *has, have*   no simple solutions.

   9. Most advertisements are directed toward adults and teenagers, but you can see commercials on television that   *is, are*   aimed at prompting children to persuade their parents to buy certain products.

   10. The requirements of the school as written in the catalog   *states, state*   that all students who   *wishes, wish*   to attend must take an entrance exam.

◇ **PRACTICE 9. Punctuating adjective clauses. (Chart 13-10)**
   Directions: Circle YES if the adjective clause requires commas and add them in the appropriate places. Circle NO if the adjective clause does not require commas.

   1. YES (NO) I made an appointment with a doctor who is considered an expert on eye disorders.
   2. (YES) NO I made an appointment with Dr. Raven, who is considered an expert on eye disorders.
   3. YES NO The car that Al bought had had three previous owners, but it was in excellent condition.
   4. YES NO We thoroughly enjoyed the music which we heard at the concert last Sunday.

5. YES NO Bogota which is the capital of Colombia is a cosmopolitan city.

6. YES NO They climbed Mount Rainier which is in the State of Washington twice last year.

7. YES NO Emeralds which are valuable gemstones are mined in Colombia.

8. YES NO The company offered the position to John whose department performed best this year.

9. YES NO On our trip to Africa we visited Nairobi which is near several fascinating game reserves and then traveled to Egypt to see the pyramids.

10. YES NO I think the waiter who took our order used to work at Captain Bob's Restaurant.

11. YES NO Someone who understands physics better than I do is going to have to help you.

12. YES NO Larry was very close to his only brother who was a famous social historian.

13. YES NO Violent tropical storms that occur in western Asia are called typhoons.

14. YES NO Similar storms that occur on the Atlantic side of the Americas are called hurricanes rather than typhoons.

15. YES NO A typhoon which is a violent tropical storm can cause great destruction.

16. YES NO According to the news report, the typhoon that threatened to strike the Indonesian coast has moved away from land and toward open water.

◇ **PRACTICE 10. Punctuating adjective clauses. (Chart 13-10)**
Directions: Choose the correct answer or answers.

1. Ms. Donaldson, ____*A*____ teaches linguistics at the university, recently received recognition for her research on the use of gestures in communication.
   A. who   B. whom   C. which   D. that   E. Ø

2. A woman ____*A, D*____ teaches linguistics at the university received an award for outstanding research.
   A. who   B. whom   C. which   D. that   E. Ø

3. The earth, _____ is the fifth largest planet in the solar system, is the third planet from the sun.
   A. who   B. whom   C. which   D. that   E. Ø

4. A grant of $1.5 million was awarded to Dr. Sato, _____ has impressed the scientific community with his research on the common cold.
   A. who   B. whom   C. which   D. that   E. Ø

5. The award for the Most Valuable Player was won by a player _____ the coaches and the entire team respect.
   A. who   B. whom   C. which   D. that   E. Ø

6. The award was won by Dennis Johnson, _____ the coach highly respects.
   A. who   B. whom   C. which   D. that   E. Ø

7. My accountant, _____ understands the complexities of the tax system, is doing my taxes this year.
   A. who   B. whom   C. which   D. that   E. Ø

8. The school board voted to close a neighborhood elementary school. The decision, _____ affected over 200 students, was not warmly received in the community.
   A. who   B. whom   C. which   D. that   E. Ø

9. Our office needs a secretary _____ knows how to use various word processing programs.
   A. who   B. whom   C. which   D. that   E. Ø

10. The winner of the Nobel Prize in physics dedicated the honor to his high school physics teacher, _____ had been an inspiration during his early years.
    A. who   B. whom   C. which   D. that   E. Ø

11. The consultant _____ was hired to advise us never really understood our situation.
    A. who   B. whom   C. which   D. that   E. Ø

12. I gave the check to Oliver, _____ promptly cashed it and spent all the money before the day was out.
    A. who   B. whom   C. which   D. that   E. Ø

13. The check _____ I gave Oliver was for work he'd done for me.
    A. who   B. whom   C. which   D. that   E. Ø

◇ **PRACTICE 11. Punctuating adjective clauses. (Chart 13-10)**
   Directions: Choose the correct explanation of the meaning of each sentence.

1. The students, who attend class five hours per day, have become quite proficient in their new language.
   (a.) *All* of the students attend class for five hours per day.
   b. *Only some* of the students attend class for five hours per day.

2. The students who attend class five hours per day have become quite proficient in their new language.
   a. *All* of the students attend class for five hours per day.
   (b.) *Only some* of the students attend class for five hours per day.

3. The orchestra conductor signaled the violinists, who were to begin playing.
   a. *All* of the violinists were to begin playing.
   b. *Only some* of the violinists were to begin playing.

4. The orchestra conductor signaled the violinists who were to begin playing.
   a. *All* of the violinists were to begin playing.
   b. *Only some* of the violinists were to begin playing.

5. I put the vase on top of the TV set, which is in the living room.
   a. I have *more than one* TV set.
   b. I have *only one* TV set.

6. I put the vase on top of the TV set that is in the living room.
   a. I have *more than one* TV set.
   b. I have *only one* TV set.

7. Trees which lose their leaves in winter are called deciduous trees.
   a. *All* trees lose their leaves in winter.
   b. *Only some* trees lose their leaves in winter.

8. Pine trees, which are evergreen, grow well in a cold climate.
   a. *All* pine trees are evergreen.
   b. *Only some* pine trees are evergreen.

◇ **PRACTICE 12. Punctuating adjective clauses. (Charts 13-10 → 13-13)**

Directions: Circle YES if the adjective clause requires commas and add the commas in the appropriate places. Circle NO if the adjective clause does not require commas.

1. (YES) NO   Thirty people, two of whom were members of the crew, were killed in the ferry accident.

2. YES (NO)   I'm trying to convince my mother to buy a small car which has front-wheel drive instead of a large car with rear-wheel drive.

3. YES NO   Over 500 students took the entrance examination the results of which will be posted in the administration building at the end of the month.

4. YES NO   The newspapers carried the story of an accident in which four pedestrians were injured.

5. YES NO   The newly married couple that lives next door just moved here from California.

6. YES NO   The new supervisor was not happy with his work crew none of whom seemed interested in doing quality work.

7. YES NO   My oldest brother in whose house I lived for six months when I was ten has been a father to me in many ways.

8. YES NO   Tom is always interrupting me which makes me mad.

9. YES NO   To express the uselessness of worrying, Mark Twain once said, "I've had a lot of problems in my life most of which never happened."

◇ **PRACTICE 13. Expressions of quantity in adjective clauses. (Chart 13-11)**

Directions: Combine the sentences. Use the second sentence as an adjective clause.

1. I received two job offers. I accepted neither of them.
   → *I received two job offers, neither of which I accepted.*

2. I have three brothers. Two of them are professional athletes.

3. Jerry is engaged in several business ventures. Only one of them is profitable.

4. The United States of America is a union of fifty states. The majority of them are located east of the Mississippi River.

5. The two women have already dissolved their business partnership. Both of them are changing careers.

6. Tom is proud of his success. Much of it has been due to hard work, but some of it has been due to good luck.

◇ **PRACTICE 14. Adjective phrases. (Charts 13-14 and 13-15)**

Directions: Change the adjective clauses to adjective phrases.

1. Only a few of the movies that are shown at the Gray Theater are suitable for children.
   → *Only a few of the movies shown at the Gray Theater are suitable for children.*

2. We visited Madrid, which is the capital of Spain..
   → *We visited Madrid, the capital of Spain.*

3. The couple who live in the house next door are both college professors.

4. Astronomy, which is the study of planets and stars, is one of the world's oldest sciences.

5. Only a small fraction of the eggs that are laid by a fish actually hatch and survive to adulthood.

6. Jasmine, which is a viny plant with fragrant flowers, grows only in warm places.

7. Arizona, which was once thought to be a useless desert, is today a rapidly growing industrial and agricultural state.

8. Simon Bolivar, who was a great South American general, led the fight for independence early in the 19th century.

9. In hot weather, many people enjoy lemonade, which is a drink that is made from lemon juice, water, and sugar.

10. I was awakened by the sound of laughter which came from the room which was next to mine at the motel.

11. Few tourists ever see a jaguar, which is a spotted wild cat that is native to tropical America.

◇ **PRACTICE 15. Punctuating adjective phrases. (Charts 13-14 and 13-15)**
Directions: Add commas where necessary.

1. A national holiday has been established in memory of Martin Luther King, Jr. the leader of the civil rights movement in the United States in the 1950s and 1960s.

2. Neil Armstrong the first person to set foot on the moon reported that the surface was fine and powdery.

3. Mark Twain is an author known far and wide as one of the greatest American humorists.

4. Susan B. Anthony one of the first leaders of the campaign for women's rights worked tirelessly during her lifetime to gain the right to vote for women.

◇ **PRACTICE 16. Adjective phrases. (Charts 13-14 and 13-15)**
Directions: Combine the sentences. Use the second sentence as an adjective phrase.

1. Louisville was founded in 1778. It is the largest city in Kentucky.
   → *Louisville, the largest city in Kentucky, was founded in 1778.*

2. John Quincy Adams was born on July 11, 1767. He was the sixth president of the United States.

3. Two languages, Finnish and Swedish, are used in Helsinki. It is the capital of Finland.

4. The Washington National Monument is a famous landmark in the nation's capital. It is a towering obelisk made of white marble.

5. Honolulu has consistently pleasant weather. It is best known to the traveler for Waikiki Beach.

6. Libya is a leading producer of oil. It is a country in North Africa.

◇ **PRACTICE 17. Adjective phrases. (Charts 13-14 and 13-15)**
Directions: Change all of the adjective clauses to adjective phrases.

1. None of the pedestrians who were walking up and down the busy street stopped to help or even inquire about the elderly man who was slumped in the doorway of an apparently unoccupied building.
   → *None of the pedestrians walking up and down the busy street stopped to help or even inquire about the elderly man slumped in the doorway of an apparently unoccupied building.*

2. Food that passes from the mouth to the stomach goes through a tube which is called the esophagus.

3. Animals that are born in a zoo generally adjust to captivity better than those that are captured in the wild.

4. The children attended a special movie program that consisted of cartoons that featured Donald Duck and Mickey Mouse.

5. One of the most important foodstuffs in the world is flour, which is a fine powder that is made by grinding wheat or other grains.

6. Nero, who was Emperor of Rome from A.D. 54 to 68, is believed to have murdered both his mother and his wife.

7. The conclusion which is presented in that book states that most of the automobiles which are produced by American industry in the 1960s and '70s had some defect.

8. Pictures that showed the brutality of war entered the living rooms of millions of TV watchers on the nightly news.

9. The Indians who lived in Peru before the discovery of the New World by Europeans belonged to the Incan culture.

10. My uncle Elias, who is a restaurant owner, often buys fish and shellfish from boats that are docked at the local pier. Customers come from miles around to dine on a seafood feast that is considered to be the best in all of the northeastern United States.

11. Hundreds of volunteers went to a northern village yesterday to reinforce firefighters who are trying to save a settlement which is threatened by a forest fire. The fire started when a cigarette ignited oil which was leaking from a machine which is used to cut timber.

12. Researchers have developed a way to mark genes so that they glow in the dark, which is a technique that scientists can use to follow specific genetic activity of cells which are within plants and animals. This development, which was announced by the National Science Foundation, which is the sponsor of the research, should prove useful to scientists who study the basic functions of organisms.

◇ **PRACTICE 18. Error analysis: adjective clauses and phrases. (Charts 13-2 → 13-15)**
Directions: All of the following sentences contain errors in adjective clauses, adjective phrases, or punctuation. Find the errors and correct them, using any appropriate form.

1. When we walked past the theater, there were a lot of people waited in a long line outside the box office.

2. Students who living on campus are close to their classrooms and the library.

3. If you need any information, see the librarian sits at the central desk on the second floor.

4. My oldest sister is Anna is 21 years old.

5. Hiroko was born in Sapporo that is a city in Japan.

6. Patrick who is my oldest brother. He is married and has one child.

7. The person sits next to me is someone I've never met him.

8. My favorite place in the world is a small city is located on the southern coast of Brazil.

9. Last Saturday I attended a party giving by one of my friends. My friend, who his apartment is in another town, was very glad I could come.

10. Dr. Darnell was the only person to whom I wanted to see.

11. There are eighty students, are from all over the world, study English at this school.

12. The people who we met them on our trip last May are going to visit us in October.

13. Dianne Jones that used to teach Spanish has organized a tour of Central America for senior citizens.

14. I've met many people since I came here who some of them are from my country.

15. People can speak English can be understood in many countries.

◇ PRACTICE 19. TEST A: Adjective clauses. (Chapter 13)

Directions: Choose the correct answer.

Example: Friends are people __B__ close to us.
  A. who is   B. who are   C. which is   D. which are

1. "Who is eligible for the scholarship?"
   "Anyone _____ scholastic record is above average can apply for the scholarship."
   A. who has a   B. has a   C. who's a   D. whose

2. Dr. Sales is a person _____.
   A. in whom I don't have much confidence   C. whom I don't have much confidence in him
   B. in that I don't have much confidence   D. I don't have much confidence

3. "Is April twenty-first the day _____?"
   "No, the twenty-second."
   A. you'll arrive then   C. on that you'll arrive
   B. when you'll arrive   D. when you'll arrive on

4. The severe drought _____ occurred last summer ruined the corn crop.
   A. that it   B. which it   C. it   D. that

5. Florida, _____ the Sunshine State, attracts many tourists every year.
   A. is   B. known as   C. is known as   D. that is known as

6. The new shopping mall is gigantic. It's advertised as a place _____ you can find just about anything you might want to buy.
   A. where   B. which   C. in where   D. in that

7. Lola's marriage has been arranged by her family. She is marrying a man _____.
   A. that she hardly knows him   C. she hardly knows
   B. whom she hardly knows him   D. she hardly knows him

8. People who exercise frequently have greater physical endurance than those _____.
   A. who doesn't   B. that doesn't   C. which don't   D. who don't

9. "Is this the address to _____ you want the package sent?"
   A. where   B. that   C. which   D. whom

10. Ann quit her job at the advertising agency, _____ surprised everyone.
    A. which   B. that   C. who   D. that it

11. That book is by a famous anthropologist. It's about the people in Samoa _____ for two years.
    A. that she lived   C. among whom she lived
    B. that she lived among them   D. where she lived among them

12. The missing man's family is desperately seeking anyone _____ information about his activities.
    A. has   B. having   C. who have   D. have

13. The publishers expect that the new biography of Simon Bolivar will be bought by people _____ in Latin American history.
    A. who are interested
    B. are interested
    C. interested
    D. they are interested

14. I have always wanted to visit Paris, _____ of France.
    A. is the capital
    B. which the capital is
    C. that is the capital
    D. the capital

15. The chemistry book _____ was a little expensive.
    A. that I bought it   B. I bought that   C. what I bought   D. I bought

16. "Have you ever met the man _____ over there?"
    "No. Who is he?"
    A. stands
    B. standing
    C. is standing
    D. who he is standing

17. "Do you have the book _____ the teacher?"
    "Yes, I do."
    A. that it belongs to
    B. to which belongs to
    C. to which belongs
    D. that belongs to

18. The voters were overwhelmingly against the candidate _____ proposals called for higher taxes.
    A. who his   B. whose   C. whom he had   D. that his

19. "Do you remember Mrs. Goddard, _____ taught us English composition?"
    "I certainly do."
    A. who   B. whom   C. that   D. which

20. I have three brothers, _____ are businessmen.
    A. that all of them
    B. who they all
    C. all of whom
    D. who all of them

◇ **PRACTICE 20. TEST B: Adjective clauses. (Chapter 13)**
Directions: Choose the correct answer.

Example: Friends are people __B__ close to us.

    A. who is   B. who are   C. which is   D. which are

1. "Were you able to locate the person _____ wallet you found?"
   "Luckily, yes."
    A. which   B. that his   C. whose   D. that's

2. Some fish is frozen, but _____ is best.
    A. fish is fresh   C. fish fresh
    B. fresh fish   D. fresh fish is caught

3. "Why do you get up at 4:00 A.M.?"
   "Because it's the only time _____ without being interrupted."
    A. when I can work on my book   C. when I can work on my book then
    B. when I can work on my book at   D. at when I can work on my book

4. "You seem so happy today."
   "I am. You are looking at a person _____ has just been accepted into medical school!"
    A. who   B. who she   C. whom she   D. whom

5. "The movie _____ last night was terrific."
   "What's it about?"
    A. I went   B. I went to it   C. I went to   D. that I went

6. Many people lost their homes in the earthquake. The government needs to establish more shelters to care for those _____ have homes.
    A. who doesn't   B. who don't   C. which doesn't   D. which don't

7. The problem _____ never occurred.
    A. I hadn't expected it   C. that I had expected it
    B. who I had expected   D. I had expected

8. I had to drive to the factory to pick up my brother, _____ car wouldn't start.
    A. who his   B. who   C. who's   D. whose

9. I read a book about Picasso, _____.
    A. is a Spanish painter   C. who a Spanish painter is
    B. a Spanish painter   D. that is a Spanish painter

10. The people _____ the acrobat turn circles in the air were horrified when he missed the outstretched hands of his partner and fell to his death.
    A. watched   B. watch   C. watching   D. were watching

11. "My writing has improved a lot in this class."
   "Mine has, too. All the students _____ do well in writing."
    A. whom Mr. Davis teaches them   C. that Mr. Davis teaches them
    B. which Mr. Davis teaches   D. Mr. Davis teaches

12. "Have you seen the place _____ the graduation ceremony will be held?"
    "Yes. It's big enough to hold 5,000 people."
       A. in that   B. where   C. is where that   D. which

13. "How's your class this term?"
    "Great. I have seventeen students, most of _____ speak English very well."
       A. who   B. those   C. whom   D. which

14. "Will everyone like the book?"
    "No. Only people _____ interested in anthropology."
       A. are   B. who are   C. in whom are   D. that is

15. "How did you enjoy your dinner with Mr. Jackson?"
    "It was boring. He talked only about himself, _____ almost put us to sleep."
       A. which   B. that   C. who   D. that he

16. My grandfather, _____ a wise man, has greatly influenced my life.
       A. is   B. that is   C. who is   D. who he is

17. "Is Dr. Brown the person _____ you wish to speak?"
    "Yes, please."
       A. that   B. whom   C. to that   D. to whom

18. In the movie, a teenager _____ to pursue a singing career meets resistance from his strong-willed father.
       A. wants   B. wanted   C. wanting   D. who want

19. "Excuse me, but there is something about _____ immediately."
    "Certainly."
       A. which I must speak to you   C. that I must speak to you about
       B. which I must speak to you about it   D. that I must speak to you

20. *Little Women,* _____ in 1868, is my sister's favorite book.
       A. is a novel published   C. a novel was published
       B. a novel published   D. was a novel published

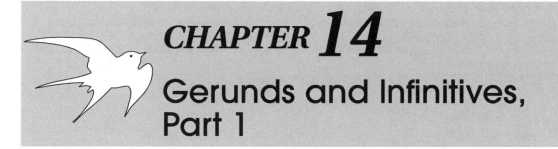

CHAPTER 14
Gerunds and Infinitives, Part 1

◇ **PRACTICE 1. Gerunds as objects of prepositions. (Chart 14-2)**
   Directions: Complete the sentences with prepositions followed by gerunds. Use the verbs in the
   given list. Use each verb only once.

✓ask	have	make	see
break	kill	open	talk
finish	lock	practice	wash

1. Instead __of asking__ for help on each arithmetic problem, you should use your book and
   try to figure out the answers yourself.

2. I look forward _____ you next time I'm in town. I'll be sure to let you
   know ahead of time so that we can plan to get together.

3. Alice told us that she was tired _____ the dishes every night.

4. The four-year-old was blamed _____ the glass candy dish.

5. Because of the bomb scare, no one was allowed in the building. People were prevented
   _____ the front door by a guard who was stationed there.

6. You should listen to other people instead _____ about yourself all the
   time.

7. What do you feel _____ for dinner? Does chicken and rice sound good?

8. Frank is an environmentalist who believes animals should be protected from hunters. He
   objects _____ wild animals for sport.

9. Please don't argue _____ your homework. Just do it.

10. Marie is responsible _____ all the doors and windows and
    _____ sure all the lights are turned off before she leaves work in the
    evening.

11. Mario spent all month preparing for the tennis match, but in spite _____
    for many hours each day, he lost the match to Ivan.

◇ **PRACTICE 2. Gerunds as objects of prepositions. (Charts 14-2 and 14-3)**
Directions: Complete the sentences in column A with the ideas in column B. Be sure to link them with an appropriate preposition.

Example: I thanked my classmate . . . .
　　　→ *I thanked my classmate for helping me with my homework.*

Column A	**Column B**
1. I thanked my classmate	A. answer students' questions
2. The treasurer is responsible	B. get a new doll for her birthday
3. The students complained	✔C. help me with my homework
4. I apologized	D. lift heavy weights
5. A bodybuilder is capable	E. get me a pillow
6. A teacher is used*	F. step on my friend's toe
7. The rainy weather prevented us	G. enter a military base
8. All of the children participated	H. balance the checkbook
9. Unauthorized persons are prohibited	I. be forced to work overtime
10. The little girl was excited	J. go on a picnic
11. I thanked the flight attendant	K. have too many tests
12. The employees objected	L. make decorations for their classroom

◇ **PRACTICE 3. Verbs followed by gerunds. (Charts 14-4 and 14-5)**
Directions: Make sentences using the given verbs.

Examples: enjoy + watch → *Do you enjoy watching old movies on television?*
　　　　　mind + have to be → *I don't mind having to be in class at 8:00 A.M.*
　　　　　put off + pack → *Dan usually puts off packing his suitcase until the very last minute.*

1. enjoy + take
2. avoid + eat
3. go + jog
4. finish + do
5. suggest + change
6. consider + go + swim
7. stop + cry
8. discuss + go + shop
9. mention + have to go
10. delay + put
11. mind + take
12. keep + ask
13. quit + worry about
14. postpone + take

---

*COMPARE:
Used + **to** + **-ing** means "accustomed to doing something."
　*Mary is **used to living** in a cold climate. = Mary is accustomed to living in a cold climate.*
Used + **to** + simple form (infinitive) expresses habitual past activities.
　*Jack **used to live** in Chicago. = Jack lived in Chicago in the past, but now he doesn't.*

◇ **PRACTICE 4. Special expressions followed by -ing. (Chart 14-6)**
Directions: Combine the given ideas into one sentence.

1. play soccer . . . spend . . . all yesterday afternoon . . . we
   → *We spent all yesterday afternoon playing soccer.*
2. a really good time . . . all of us . . . have . . . play soccer in the park . . . yesterday
3. find . . . have trouble . . . Omar . . . my house . . . last night
4. my bicycle . . . my mother . . . try to steal . . . catch . . . some neighborhood kids . . . yesterday
5. at the window . . . stand . . . when the boss walked into the office . . . all of the employees . . . watch the parade on the street below
6. my father always said, ". . . read novels . . . your time . . . from other kinds of books . . . when you could be learning something worthwhile . . . don't waste"
7. when Mrs. Smith checked on the children last night . . . play a game . . . find . . . instead of sleeping . . . them . . . she
8. Susan . . . find . . . when I opened the door . . . I . . . on her bed . . . cry . . . lie

◇ **PRACTICE 5. Gerund vs. infinitive. (Charts 14-1 → 14-7)**
Directions: Select the correct answer for each sentence.

1. Whenever we met, Jack avoided ___B___ at me.
   A. to look   B. looking

2. Most people enjoy _____ to different parts of the world.
   A. to travel   B. traveling

3. Marjorie needs _____ another job. Her present company is going out of business.
   A. to find   B. finding

4. May I change the TV channel, or do you want _____ more of this program?
   A. to watch   B. watching

5. Joan is considering _____ her major from pre-med studies to psychology.
   A. to change   B. changing

6. Although Joe slammed on his brakes, he couldn't avoid _____ the small dog that suddenly darted out in front of his car.
   A. to hit   B. hitting

7. I hope _____ my autobiography before I die. Do you think anyone would read it?
   A. to write   B. writing

8. Joyce thanked us for _____ them to dinner and said that they wanted to have us over for dinner next week.
   A. to invite   B. inviting

9. If you delay _____ your bills, you will only incur more and more interest charges.
   A. to pay   B. paying

10. My lawyer advised me not _____ anything further about the accident.
    A. to say   B. saying

11. A procrastinator is one who habitually postpones _____ things — especially tasks that are unpleasant.
    A. to do   B. doing

12. You should plan _____ at the stadium early or you won't be able to get good seats.
    A. to arrive   B. arriving

13. My mom asked me _____ up some eggs at the supermarket on my way home from work.
    A. to pick   B. picking

14. Nobody has offered _____ the house next door, so I think they're going to lower the price.
    A. to buy   B. buying

15. The highway patrol advises _____ the old route through the city because the interstate highway is under major repairs.
    A. to take   B. taking

16. Would you mind _____ that apple for me? My arthritis is acting up in my right hand.
    A. to peel   B. peeling

17. Stop _____ me! I'll get everything finished before I go to bed.
    A. to nag   B. nagging

18. When the university suggested _____ the tuition again, the student senate protested vigorously.
    A. to raise   B. raising

19. Are we permitted _____ guests to the ceremony? I'd like to invite my friend to join us.
    A. to bring   B. bringing

20. The city council agreed _____ the architect's proposed design for a new parking garage.
    A. to accept   B. accepting

◇ **PRACTICE 6. Verbs followed by infinitives. (Chart 14-7)**
    Directions: Restate the given sentences. Choose the most appropriate reporting verb in parentheses. Make it active or passive as appropriate. Include an infinitive in the completion and any other necessary words.

    1. The teacher said to Jim, "Would you give your book to Mary, please?"
       (ask, tell, order)
       → The teacher ___asked Jim to give___ his book to Mary.

    2. The sign said, "No parking in this area. Violators will be towed away."
       (invite, warn, force)
       → Drivers ___were warned not to park___ in the area.

    3. Before Bobby went to bed, his father said, "Don't forget to brush your teeth."
       (invite, allow, remind)
       → Before Bobby went to bed, his father _____ his teeth.

    4. Under the law, drivers and all passengers must wear seat belts while in a moving vehicle.
       (encourage, require, permit)
       → Drivers and passengers _____ seat belts while in a moving vehicle.

5. When I asked the nurse about my skin rash, she said, "You should consult a dermatologist."
   (ask, permit, advise)
   → The nurse _____ a dermatologist.

6. The fire chief said, "Everyone must leave the building immediately."
   (order, remind, allow)
   → Everyone _____ the building immediately.

7. The instructor said to the students, "You will have exactly one hour to complete the exam."
   (order, expect, warn)
   → The students _____ the exam in one hour.

8. Because he forgot last year, I told my husband several times that he should buy some flowers for his mother on Mother's Day.
   (remind, require, allow)
   → I _____ some flowers for his mother on Mother's Day.

9. My garage mechanic said, "You should get a tune-up every 5,000 miles."
   (ask, order, advise)
   → My garage mechanic _____ a tune-up every 5,000 miles.

10. The factory manager said to the employees, "Do not come late. If you do, you will lose your jobs."
    (ask, warn, encourage)
    → The employees _____ late.

11. The sign on the side door says, "Do not enter," so we have to use a different door.
    (ask, permit, force)
    → Nobody _____ the side door.

12. The little girl said to her father, "Daddy, I really like this tricycle. Can we buy it?"
    (require, ask, advise)
    → The little girl _____ the tricycle for her.

13. We often told our grandfather, "Your experiences as a sailor in the navy were fascinating. You should write a book about them."
    (remind, encourage, require)
    → We _____ a book about his experiences in the navy.

14. The judge said to the defendant, "You must not shout in the courtroom again."
    (ask, order, encourage)
    → The defendant _____ in the courtroom again.

◇ **PRACTICE 7. Verbs followed by infinitives. (Chart 14-7)**
   Directions: Report what the speakers say by using a verb from the following list and an infinitive phrase. Use each verb in the list only once. Make your sentence passive if the speaker is not specifically identified.

advise	✔ask	invite	remind
allow	encourage	order	warn

1. During the water shortage, someone in authority said to the public, "Curtail your use of water as much as possible."
   → *During the water shortage, the public was asked to curtail its use of water as much as possible.*

2. Laura said to her roommate, "Don't forget to set your alarm clock for 6:00."

3. Mrs. Jones said to the children, "Each of you may have one piece of candy."

4. The doctor said to my father, "It would be best if you limited your sugar consumption."

5. My parents often said to me, "Good for you! It's good to be independent!"

6. Someone said to the children, "Don't swim in the lake without an adult present."

7. The police officer shouted to the reckless driver, "Pull over!"

8. Rose said to Jerry, "I'd like you to come to my house Sunday night to meet my parents."

◇ **PRACTICE 8. Gerund vs. infinitive. (Chart 14-8)**
Directions: Choose the best answer or answers. In some cases, BOTH answers are correct.

1. John was trying —— B —— the door with the wrong key.
   A. unlocking   B. to unlock

2. The audience began —— A, B —— before the curtains closed.
   A. clapping   B. to clap

3. The soccer teams continued _____ even though it began to snow.
   A. playing   B. to play

4. We like _____ outside when the weather is warm and sunny.
   A. eating   B. to eat

5. We began _____ to the news when we heard the Olympics mentioned.
   A. listening   B. to listen

6. I was just beginning _____ asleep when the phone rang.
   A. falling   B. to fall

7. I really hate _____ late for appointments.
   A. being   B. to be

8. The cake was starting _____ when I took it out of the oven.
   A. burning   B. to burn

9. She's so impatient! She can't stand _____ in line for anything.
   A. waiting   B. to wait

10. I prefer _____ my bicycle to work because the automobile traffic is too heavy.
    A. riding   B. to ride

11. Lillian prefers _____ to taking the bus.
    A. walking   B. to walk

12. Tim prefers _____ than to jog for exercise.
    A. walking   B. to walk

13. The baby loves _____ in the car.
    A. riding   B. to ride

14. Near the end of the performance, the audience began _____ their feet on the floor.
    A. stamping   B. to stamp

15. The audience began to clap and _____ their feet on the floor.
    A. stamping   B. (to) stamp

16. The audience began clapping and _____ their feet on the floor.
    A. stamping   B. (to) stamp

17. My son sometimes forgets _____ the stove when he is finished cooking.
    A. turning off   B. to turn off

18. Alex will never forget _____ his first helicopter ride.
    A. taking   B. to take

19. Would you please remember _____ away all the tapes when you're finished listening to them?
    A. putting   B. to put

20. I remember _____ them away when I finished with them last night.
    A. putting   B. to put

21. I remember _____ Bolivia for the first time. It's a beautiful country.
    A. visiting   B. to visit

22. What am I going to do? I forgot _____ my calculus text, and I need it for the review today.
    A. bringing   B. to bring

23. My boss regrets _____ his secretary now that she is gone.
    A. firing   B. to fire

24. The letter said, "I regret _____ you that your application has been denied."
    A. informing   B. to inform

25. I haven't been able to get in touch with Shannon. I tried _____ her. Then I tried _____ her a letter. I tried _____ a message with her brother when I talked to him. Nothing worked.
    A. calling . . . writing . . . leaving   B. to call . . . to write . . . to leave

26. I always try _____ my bills on time, but sometimes I'm a little late.
    A. paying   B. to pay

◇ **PRACTICE 9. Gerund vs. infinitive. (Charts 14-9 and 14-10)**
    Directions: Work with another person. One of you should read the beginning of the sentence, and the other, without looking at the book, should supply the correct response: ***to do it*** or ***doing it***. (If you are studying alone, cover up the answers in parentheses and check yourself as you go.)

    Example: A: I enjoy . . . .
              B: . . . doing it.
    1. I dislike .... (doing it.)
    2. She was ordered .... (to do it.)
    3. I urged my friend .... (to do it.)
    4. Can he afford .... (to do it?)

5. We all discussed .... (doing it.)

6. The institute requires us .... (to do it.)

7. We will eventually complete .... (doing it.)

8. The whole class practiced .... (doing it.)

9. I really don't care .... (to do it.)

10. My friend recommended not .... (doing it.)

11. She was expected .... (to do it.)

12. Bill resented his roommate .... (doing it.)

13. Did the criminal admit .... (doing it?)

14. Please allow us .... (to do it.)

15. The whole family anticipated .... (doing it.)

16. No one recollected .... (doing it.)

17. Did you risk .... (doing it?)

18. Did they recall .... (doing it?)

19. My friend challenged me .... (to do it.)

20. The teacher postponed .... (doing it.)

21. Do you mind .... (doing it?)

22. Why did he pretend .... (to do it?)

23. The teacher arranged .... (to do it.)

24. The regulations permit us .... (to do it.)

25. The dentist wanted to delay .... (doing it.)

26. Can anyone learn .... (to do it?)

27. Did your roommate offer .... (to do it?)

28. He doesn't deny .... (doing it.)

29. Somehow, the dog managed .... (to do it.)

30. Everyone avoided .... (doing it.)

31. The boy dared Al .... (to do it.)

32. Our teacher threatened .... (to do it.)

33. The contestant practiced .... (doing it.)

34. My friend consented .... (to do it.)

35. I miss .... (doing it.)

◇ **PRACTICE 10. Gerund vs. infinitive. (Charts 14-2 → 14-10)**
Directions: Complete the sentences with the correct form, gerund or infinitive, using the words in parentheses.

1. The store offered __to refund__ the money I paid for the book I returned. *(refund)*

2. Don't pretend __to be__ what you aren't. *(be)*

3. I persuaded my brother-in-law not _____ that old car. *(buy)*

4. Annie denied _____ the brick through the window. *(throw)*

5. My father expects me _____ high marks in school. *(get)*

6. According to the sign on the restaurant door, all diners are required _____ shirts and shoes. *(wear)*

7. We are planning _____ several historical sites in Moscow. *(visit)*

8. There appears _____ no way to change our reservation for the play at this late date. *(be)*

9. For some strange reason, I keep _____ today is Saturday. *(think)*

10. All of the members agreed _____ the emergency meeting. *(attend)*

11. I've arranged _____ work early tomorrow. *(leave)*

12. Even though Anna had never cut anyone's hair before, she readily consented _____ her husband's hair. *(cut)*

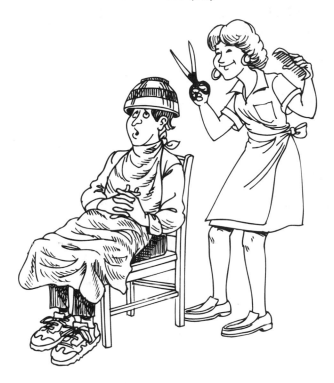

13. Mary decided _____ her friend's critical remarks. *(ignore)*

14. My roommate says I have a terrible voice, so I stopped _____ in the shower. *(sing)*

15. Did the doctor mention _____ any foods in particular? *(avoid)*

16. The cashier always remembers _____ the money in her cash register each day before she leaves work. *(count)*

17. Let's hurry! We must finish _____ the office before 3:00 today. *(paint)*

18. The student with the highest average deserves _____ an "A." *(get)*

19. I appreciate your _____ for my dinner. I'll buy next time. *(pay)*

20. The physically handicapped child struggled _____ up with the other children on the playground, but she couldn't. *(keep)*

21. Janice misses _____ walks with her father in the evening now that she has moved away from home. *(take)*

22. The customs official demanded _____ what was inside the gift-wrapped box. *(know)*

23. We've discussed _____ to New York in the fall, but I'm worried about our children having to adjust to a new school system and new friends. *(move)*

24. Children shouldn't be allowed _____ violent programs on TV. *(watch)*

25. In a fit of anger, I ordered my neighbor _____ his mule off my property. *(keep)*

◇ **PRACTICE 11. Gerund vs. infinitive. (Charts 14-2 → 14-10)**
   Directions: Complete the sentences with the correct form, gerund or infinitive, using the words in parentheses.

1. The doctor was forced ___to operate___ immediately to save the patient's life. *(operate)*

2. The newspaper hired Bill _____ pictures of the championship match between the two boxers. *(shoot)*

3. Most passengers dislike _____ to sit in small, uncomfortable seats on transoceanic flights. *(have)*

4. I choose _____ to Stanford University for my undergraduate studies. *(go)*

5. I must drive more carefully. I can't risk _____ another speeding ticket. *(get)*

6. All of the members agreed _____ the emergency meeting. *(attend)*

7. Jack promised _____ to the meeting. *(come)*

8. The sign warns you not _____ right on a red light. *(turn)*

9. Did Dick mean _____ Sue about the surprise party, or did it slip out accidentally? *(tell)*

10. You must keep _____ on the computer until you understand how to use all of the programs. *(practice)*

11. Our class volunteered _____ the classroom during the maintenance workers' strike. *(clean)*

12. When you get through _____ the newspaper, I could use your help in the kitchen. *(read)*

13. I think we should delay _____ these reports to the main office. *(send)*

14. The judge demanded _____ the original document, not the photocopy. *(see)*

15. After hearing the weather report, I advise you not _____ skiing this afternoon. *(go)*

16. George is interested in _____ an art class. *(take)*

17. I was furious. I threatened never _____ to him again. *(speak)*

18. My parents appreciated _____ the thank-you note you sent them. *(receive)*

19. The committee is planning _____ next Friday. *(meet)*

20. If I don't leave on the 15th, I will miss _____ home in time for my mother's birthday party. *(get)*

21. I know you're anxious to get out of here and get back home, but you should seriously consider _____ in the hospital a few more days. *(stay)*

22. Alex refused _____ for his rude behavior. *(apologize)*

23. When I was in the army, I had to swear _____ my senior officers' orders. *(obey)*

24. I don't recall _____ your dictionary anywhere in the apartment. Maybe you left it in the classroom. *(see)*

25. Mrs. Lind required the children _____ off their muddy boots before they came into the house. *(take)*

◇ **PRACTICE 12. Gerund vs. infinitive. (Charts 14-9 and 14-10)**
   Directions: Choose the correct answer.

1. The groom anticipated ___A___ the wedding ceremony.
   A. enjoying   B. to enjoy

2. The department store agreed _____ back the damaged radio.
   A. taking   B. to take

3. Would the doctor mind _____ some time talking to me after the examination?
   A. spending   B. to spend

4. We miss _____ Professor Sanders in Asian history this quarter.
   A. having   B. to have

5. Dan failed _____ the firefighter's examination and was quite upset.
   A. passing   B. to pass

6. The travelers anticipated _____ safely at their destination.
   A. arriving   B. to arrive

7. She expects _____ her baby at the new hospital.
   A. delivering   B. to deliver

8. The bad weather caused us _____ our connecting flight to Rome.
   A. missing   B. to miss

9. We dislike _____ dinner at 9:00 P.M.
   A. eating   B. to eat

10. Most of the students completed _____ their research papers on time.
    A. writing   B. to write

11. My niece hopes _____ with me to Disneyland next April.
    A. traveling   B. to travel

12. This note will remind me _____ the chicken for dinner tomorrow night.
    A. defrosting   B. to defrost

13. Willy denied _____ a whole bag of chocolate chip cookies before lunch.
    A. eating   B. to eat

14. You must swear _____ the truth in a court of law.
    A. telling   B. to tell

15. I didn't mean _____ him.
    A. interrupting   B. to interrupt

◇ **PRACTICE 13. Gerund vs. infinitive. (Charts 14-9 and 14-10)**
Directions: Create sentences from the following verb combinations. Select any tense for the first verb, but use a gerund or infinitive for the second verb. Include a (PRO)NOUN OBJECT if necessary.

Examples: can't afford + buy → *I can't afford to buy a new car for at least another year.*
           dare + dive → *My friends dared me to dive into the pool.*

1. keep + play
2. direct + save
3. regret + tell
4. manage + get
5. remind + take
6. be used to + stay
7. persuade + not buy
8. mention + give
9. suggest + go
10. can't imagine + travel
11. recommend + take
12. convince + go + swim
13. miss + be
14. not appreciate + hear
15. fail + tell
16. resent + be
17. resist + eat
18. claim + know
19. deserve + get
20. not recall + say
21. look forward to + see
22. beg + give
23. agree + hire + work
24. remember + tell + be
25. urge + practice + speak
26. tell + keep + try + call

◇ **PRACTICE 14. Using *it* + infinitive. (Chart 14-11)**

Directions: Restate the sentences by changing a sentence with a gerund as the subject to a sentence with *it* + *an infinitive phrase,* and vice-versa.

1. Teasing animals is cruel. → *It is cruel to tease animals.*

2. It wasn't difficult to find their house. → *Finding their house wasn't difficult.*

3. Voting in every election is important.

4. It was exciting to meet the king and queen.

5. Hearing the other side of the story would be interesting.

6. It is unusual to see Joan awake early in the morning.

7. If you know how, it is easy to float in the water for a long time.

8. Mastering a second language takes time and patience.

9. Driving to Atlanta will take us ten hours.

10. It takes courage to dive into the sea from a high cliff.

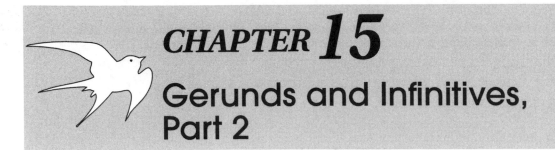

CHAPTER 15
Gerunds and Infinitives, Part 2

◇ **PRACTICE 1. In order to. (Chart 15-1)**
Directions: Add ***in order*** if possible. If nothing should be added, write **Ø**.

1. Emily likes ___Ø___ to go ice skating every weekend.

2. Please open the door ___in order___ to let some fresh air in.

3. Elizabeth has to practice at least four hours every day _____ to be ready for her piano recital next month.

4. Shelley sent me an e-mail _____ to inform me that the meeting had been canceled.

5. We've decided _____ not to take a vacation this year.

6. Did you remember _____ to call Mr. Johnson?

7. After dinner we drove to the top of a hill outside the city _____ to watch the sunset.

8. The children were making so much noise that I had to shout at them _____ to get their attention.

9. Jane is so disgusted by politics and politicians these days that she refuses _____ to vote in either local or national elections.

10. We waded across the mountain stream _____ to continue our hike to Wall's Meadow.

11. We stopped briefly on the other side of the stream _____ to rest before beginning one of the steepest parts of the climb.

12. One of the climbers hesitated _____ to continue because of a painful blister on his right heel. He tried _____ to keep up with the rest of us, but finally stopped climbing with us because of the pain.

◇ PRACTICE 2. Adjectives followed by infinitives. (Chart 15-2)

Directions: Complete the sentences with infinitives.

1. I was glad ___to get___ a letter from you.

2. I was relieved ___to find out___ that I had passed the exam.

3. Sue is lucky _____ alive after the accident.

4. The soldiers were prepared _____ .

5. The children are anxious _____ to the circus.

6. Dick didn't feel like going anywhere. He was content _____ home and
   _____ a book.

7. The teacher is always willing _____ us.

8. The students are motivated _____ English.

9. Be careful not _____ on the icy sidewalks!

10. Tom was hesitant _____ home alone on the dark street.

11. Sally is afraid _____ home alone.

12. Ann is proud _____ the top student in her class.

13. I was surprised _____ Mr. Yamamoto at the meeting.

14. We were sorry _____ thc bad news.

◇ PRACTICE 3. *Too* vs. *very.* (Chart 15-3)

Directions: Add *too* or *very* to the scntences as appropriate.

1. The box is ___very___ heavy, but I can lift it.

2. John dropped his physics course becausc it was ___too___ difficult for him.

3. I think it's _____ late to get tickets to the concert. I heard they were all sold.

4. It's _____ cold today, but I'm still going to take my daily walk.

5. Our cat is fourteen years old. Now he's _____ old to catch mice in the field across the
   street.

6. It's _____ dark to see in here. Please turn on the lights.

7. She was _____ ill. Nevertheless, she came to the family reunion.

8. The boys were _____ busy to help me clean out the garage, so I did it myself.

9. Learning a second language is _____ difficult, but most of the students are doing well.

10. We enjoyed our dinner at the restaurant last night. It was _____ good.

11. Professor Andrews is always _____ interesting, but I'm _____ tired to go to the lecture tonight.

12. He's _____ young to understand. He'll understand when he's older.

13. The meal was _____ good. I enjoyed every morsel.

14. I'm _____ sleepy to watch the rest of the TV movie. Let me know how it turns out.

15. Sally was running _____ fast for me to keep up with her, so I lagged behind.

◇ **PRACTICE 4. Using *too* and *enough*. (Chart 15-3)**
   Directions: Combine the given ideas into one sentence. Add *to* when an infinitive is required.

   1. my work . . . yesterday . . . finish . . . enough . . . not . . . time . . . have
      → *I didn't have enough time* **to** finish my work yesterday.*

   2. enough . . . not . . . well . . . go back to work . . . is . . . Linda

   3. use . . . scissors . . . too . . . are . . . for . . . sharp . . . very young children

   4. narrow . . . are . . . two-way traffic . . . the streets in the old part of the city . . . too . . . for

   5. old . . . Jimmy . . . enough . . . not . . . ride on the bus by himself . . . is

   6. many . . . in grammar and spelling in the first one . . . careless mistakes . . . Jules . . . because he had made . . . had to rewrite his composition . . . too

   7. everyone assigned to this class . . . there . . . seats in the classroom . . . are . . . enough . . . not . . . for

   8. we couldn't go . . . too . . . call the box office for tickets . . . because we waited . . . long . . . to the musical

◇ **PRACTICE 5. Passive infinitives. (Chart 15-4)**
   Directions: Choose the correct answer.

   1. When I told Tim the news, he seemed _____.
      A. to surprise   B. to be surprised

   2. The children agreed _____ the candy equally.
      A. to divide   B. to be divided

   3. Janice is going to fill out an application. She wants _____ for the job.
      A. to consider   B. to be considered

   4. The mail is supposed _____ at noon.
      A. to deliver   B. to be delivered

   5. I expect _____ at the airport by my uncle.
      A. to meet   B. to be met

_____

*Also possible: *time enough*. In everyday English, ***enough*** usually precedes the noun.

6. Mr. Steinberg offered _____ us to the train station.
   A. to drive   B. to be driven

7. The children appear _____ about the trip.
   A. to excite   B. to be excited

◇ **PRACTICE 6. Passive gerunds. (Chart 15-4)**
   Directions: Choose the correct answer.

   1. I don't appreciate _____ when I'm speaking.
      A. interrupting   B. being interrupted

   2. Avoid _____ your houseplants too much water.
      A. giving   B. being given

   3. The mountain climbers are in danger of _____ by an avalanche.
      A. killing   B. being killed

   4. Does Dr. Johnson mind _____ at home if his patients need his help?
      A. calling   B. being called

   5. I'm interested in _____ my communication skills.
      A. improving   B. being improved

   6. Mrs. Gates appreciated _____ breakfast in bed when she wasn't feeling well.
      A. serving   B. being served

   7. Sally's low test scores kept her from _____ to the university.
      A. admitting   B. being admitted

   8. Mr. Miller gave no indication of _____ his mind.
      A. changing   B. being changed

◇ **PRACTICE 7. Passive infinitives and gerunds. (Chart 15-4)**
   Directions: Choose the correct answer.

   1. Instead of _____ about the good news, Tom seemed to be indifferent.
      A. exciting   C. to excite
      B. being excited   D. to be excited

   2. The new students hope _____ in many of the school's social activities.
      A. including   C. to include
      B. being included   D. to be included

   3. The owner of the building supply store doesn't mind _____ his customers discounts when they buy in large quantities.
      A. giving   C. to give
      B. being given   D. to be given

   4. Jack got into trouble when he refused _____ his briefcase for the customs officer.
      A. opening   C. to open
      B. being opened   D. to be opened

5. Barbara didn't mention _____ about her progress report at work, but I'm sure she is.
   A. concerning
   B. being concerned
   C. to concern
   D. to be concerned

6. The City Parks Department is putting in several miles of new trails because so many people have said that they enjoy _____ on them.
   A. walking
   B. being walked
   C. to walk
   D. to be walked

7. You'd better save some money for a rainy day. You can't count on _____ by your parents every time you get into financial difficulty.
   A. rescuing
   B. being rescued
   C. to rescue
   D. to be rescued

8. Please forgive me. I didn't mean _____ you.
   A. upsetting
   B. being upset
   C. to upset
   D. to be upset

9. I don't remember _____ of the decision to change the company policy on vacations. When was it decided?
   A. telling
   B. being told
   C. to tell
   D. to be told

10. Ms. Drake expects _____ about any revisions to her manuscript before it is printed.
    A. consulting
    B. being consulted
    C. to consult
    D. to be consulted

11. Sally gave such a good speech that I couldn't resist _____ loudly when she finished.
    A. applauding
    B. being applauded
    C. to applaud
    D. to be applauded

12. Tommy admitted _____ the rock through the window.
    A. throwing
    B. being thrown
    C. to throw
    D. to be thrown

13. If you want to develop inner tranquility, you have to stop _____ by every little thing that happens.
    A. bothering
    B. being bothered
    C. to bother
    D. to be bothered

14. Paul really didn't mind _____ by the party to celebrate his fortieth birthday, although he told his friends that they shouldn't have done it.
    A. surprising
    B. being surprised
    C. to surprise
    D. to be surprised

15. Anne hopes _____ to join the private club. She could make important business contacts there.
    A. inviting
    B. being invited
    C. to invite
    D. to be invited

◇ **PRACTICE 8. Past and past-passive infinitives and gerunds. (Chart 15-4)**
   Directions: Choose the correct answer.

1. Are you sure you told me? I don't recall _____ about it.
   A. having told
   B. having been told
   C. to have told
   D. to have been told

2. Tom made a bad mistake at work, but his boss didn't fire him. He's lucky _____ a second chance.
   A. having given
   B. having been given
   C. to have given
   D. to have been given

3. Dr. Wilson is a brilliant and dedicated scientist who had expected to be selected as the director of the institute. She was very surprised not _____ the position.
   A. having offered
   B. having been offered
   C. to have offered
   D. to have been offered

4. By the time their baby arrives, the Johnsons hope _____ painting and decorating the new nursery.
   A. having finished
   B. having been finished
   C. to have finished
   D. to have been finished

5. The stockbroker denied _____ of the secret business deal.
   A. having informed
   B. having been informed
   C. to have informed
   D. to have been informed

6. The Smiths wanted to give their son every advantage. However, they now regret _____ him by providing too many material possessions.
   A. having spoiled
   B. having been spoiled
   C. to have spoiled
   D. to have been spoiled

7. The spy admitted _____ some highly secret information to enemy agents.
   A. having given
   B. having been given
   C. to have given
   D. to have been given

◇ **PRACTICE 9. Past and past-passive infinitives and gerunds. (Chart 15-4)**
   Directions: Supply an appropriate form for each verb in parentheses.

1. Sharon wants us to tell her the news as soon as we hear anything. If we find out anything about the problem, she wants *(tell)* _____ about it immediately.

2. Yesterday Anna wrote a check for fifty dollars, but when she wrote it she knew she didn't have enough money in the bank to cover it. Today she is very worried about *(write)* _____ that check. She has to find a way to put some money in her account right away.

3. A: What's the difference between "burn up" and "burn down"?

   B: Hmmm. That's an interesting question. I don't recall ever *(ask)* _____ _____ that question before.

4. Living in a foreign country has been a good experience for me. I am glad that my company sent me to another country to study. I am very pleased *(give)* _____ the opportunity to learn about another culture.

5. Martha doesn't like to have her picture taken. She avoids *(photograph)* _____ _____ .

6. A: It's been nice talking to you. I really have enjoyed our conversation, but I have to leave now. I'm very happy *(have)* _____ this opportunity to meet you and talk with you. Let's try to get together again soon.

   B: I'd like that.

7. A: This letter needs *(send)* _____ immediately. Will you take care of it?

   B: Right away.

8. Sally is very quick. You have to tell her how to do something only once. She doesn't need *(tell)* _____ twice.

9. A: I thought Sam was sick.

   B: So did I. But he seems *(recover)* _____ very quickly. He certainly doesn't seem *(be)* _____ sick now.

10. Last year I studied abroad. I appreciate *(have)* _____ the opportunity to live and study in a foreign country.

◇ **PRACTICE 10. Using a possessive to modify a gerund. (Chart 15-6)**
Directions: Combine the following. Change *that fact* to a gerund phrase. Use formal English.

Example: We answered all of the exam questions correctly. The teacher was pleased with that fact.
→ *The teacher was pleased with our answering* (OR: *having answered*) *all of the exam questions correctly.*

1. I lost my new watch. My mother was angry about that fact.
2. They are going to spend their vacation with us. We look forward to that fact.
3. Tony failed the economics test even though he studied hard. No one can understand that fact.
4. The students are required to pay an extra fee to use the laboratory. I am upset about that fact.
5. Mary worked late to finish the project. The supervisor appreciated that fact.

◇ **PRACTICE 11. Review: gerunds and infinitives. (Charts 14-1 → 15-6)**
Directions: Choose the correct answer.

1. Alice didn't expect _____ to Bill's party.
   A. asking   B. being asked   C. to ask   D. to be asked

2. I finally finished _____ at 7:00 P.M. and served dinner.
   A. cooking   B. being cooked   C. to cook   D. to be cooked

3. Sam always remembers _____ in the garage so that the driveway is free for other cars.
   A. parking   B. being parked   C. to park   D. to be parked

4. The nurse suggested _____ two aspirin.

    A. taking   B. being taken   C. to take   D. to be taken

5. Would you mind not _____ the radio until I've finished with this phone call?

    A. turning on   C. to turn on

    B. being turned on   D. to be turned on

6. They were fortunate _____ from the fire before the building collapsed.

    A. rescuing   B. to have rescued   C. to rescue   D. to have been rescued

7. The mouse family avoided _____ by coming out only when the house was empty and the two cats were outside.

    A. catching   C. to have been caught

    B. being caught   D. to be caught

8. The baby continued _____ even after she was picked up.

    A. being crying   B. having cried   C. to cry   D. having been crying

9. Arthur pretended not _____ hurt when his younger sister bit him.

    A. having   B. be   C. to have   D. to have been

10. We were shocked to hear the news of your _____.

    A. having fired   C. to be fired

    B. having been fired   D. to have been fired

11. Even though she was much younger than the other children, Alexis demanded _____ in the game they were playing.

    A. including   B. being including   C. to include   D. to be included

12. Our mechanic said that he expects _____ the brakes on the car before we pick it up.

    A. fixing   B. being fixed   C. to have fixed   D. to have been fixed

13. Marge's children are used to _____ after school every day. They don't have to walk home.

    A. picking up   B. being picked up   C. be picked up   D. pick up

14. The bus driver was so tired of _____ the same route every day that he asked for a transfer.

    A. to drive   B. being driven   C. driving   D. drive

15. I'm sure it's not my fault that Peter found out what we were planning. I don't remember _____ anyone about it.

    A. having told   B. being told   C. to tell   D. to be told

◇ **PRACTICE 12. Using verbs of perception. (Chart 15-7)**
   Directions: Complete the sentences with the words in the list. Use each word only once. Use the
   SIMPLE form or the *-ing* form, whichever seems better to you.

arrive	*emerge*	*perform*	*prevent*
chirp	*explain*	✔*practice*	*win*
climb	*melt*		

1. Whenever I have free time, I like to watch the basketball team __practice__ .

2. A few years ago, I saw a dog _____ a child from wandering into a busy
   street by standing in front of her and not letting her get by.

3. It was a thrill to see my brother _____ the chess tournament last year.

4. I was amazed to see the firefighters _____ so soon after my call.

5. The boy watched the butterfly _____ from its cocoon.

6. It is educational for children to observe adults _____ their daily tasks.

7. When I look at my gym teacher _____ the rope, it looks easy, but when
   I try it, it is hard.

8. Hearing the birds _____ tells us that spring has indeed arrived.

9. I listened to the teacher _____ how to solve the math problem.

10. I held out my hand and watched each snowflake _____ as soon as it
    touched my skin.

◇ **PRACTICE 13.** *Let, help,* and causative verbs. **(Charts 15-8 and 15-9)**
Directions: Choose the correct answer(s).

1. Instead of buying a new pair of shoes, I had my old ones ___C___ .
   A. repair   B. to repair   C. repaired

2. I helped my daughter __A, B__ her homework.
   A. finish   B. to finish   C. finished

3. I made my son _____ the windows before he could go outside to play with his friends.
   A. wash   B. to wash   C. washed

4. Maria had her landlord _____ the broken window before winter.
   A. fix   B. to fix   C. fixed

5. To please my daughter, I had her old bicycle _____ bright red.
   A. paint   B. to paint   C. painted

6. Sam was reluctant, but we finally got him _____ his guitar for us.
   A. play   B. to play   C. played

7. When I had to make an emergency phone call, the secretary let me _____ her phone.
   A. use   B. to use   C. used

8. Jack, could you help me _____ a place in the garden to plant some tomatoes?
   A. dig   B. to dig   C. dug

9. Before we leave, let's have Shelley _____ a map for us so we won't get lost.
   A. draw   B. to draw   C. drawn

10. Are you going to let me _____ that last piece of blueberry pie?
    A. eat   B. to eat   C. eaten

◇ **PRACTICE 14. Verb form review. (Charts 14-1 → 15-9)**
Directions: Choose the correct answer.

1. I enjoy _____ to the park on summer evenings.
   A. to go   B. going   C. being gone   D. go

2. Don't forget _____ home as soon as you arrive at your destination.
   A. to call   B. calling   C. having called   D. to be called

3. When I kept getting unwanted calls, I called the phone company and had my phone number
   _____ . The process was easier than I expected it to be.
   A. change   B. changed   C. to change   D. changing

4. Jean should seriously consider _____ an actress. She is a very talented performer.
   A. to become   B. become   C. becoming   D. will become

5. _____ television to the exclusion of all other activities is not a healthy habit for a growing
   child.
   A. To be watched   B. Being watched   C. Watching   D. Watch

6. After their children had grown up, Mr. and Mrs. Sills decided _____ to a condominium in the city. They've never been sorry.
   A. to have moved   B. moving   C. move   D. to move

7. I truly appreciated _____ to give the commencement address, but I wasn't able to accept the honor because of a previous commitment.
   A. asking   B. to have asked   C. to ask   D. having been asked

8. The store manager caught the cashier _____ money from the cash register and promptly called the police. They discovered that it had been going on for a long time.
   A. to sneak   B. sneaking   C. to have sneaked   D. being sneaked

9. My roommate's handwriting is very bad, so he had me _____ his paper for him last night.
   A. to type   B. type   C. to have typed   D. typed

10. The municipal authorities advised _____ all drinking water during the emergency.
    A. to boil   B. to be boiled   C. boiling   D. boil

11. If we leave now for our trip, we can drive half the distance before we stop _____ lunch.
    A. having   B. to have   C. having had   D. for having

12. Our schedule is not working out. We should discuss _____ our daily routine. I don't feel as though we're getting enough accomplished.
    A. changing   B. to change   C. to have changed   D. being changed

13. I can't recall _____ that old movie, but maybe I did many years ago.
    A. having seen   B. to have seen   C. to see   D. having been seen

14. Our school basketball team won the championship game by _____ two points in the last five seconds. It was the most exciting game I have ever attended.
    A. being scored   B. to score   C. scoring   D. score

15. The flight attendants made all the passengers _____ their seat belts during the turbulence.
    A. to buckle
    B. to have buckled
    C. buckling
    D. buckle

16. It has become necessary _____ water in the metropolitan area because of the severe drought.
    A. rationing   B. ration   C. to have rationed   D. to ration

17. You can't blame Ralph for _____ to eat that dessert. It looked delicious.
    A. to be tempted   B. tempted   C. be tempted   D. having been tempted

18. Let's leave early so we'll be ahead of the rush of commuters. We can't risk _____ in heavy traffic during rush hour.
    A. holding up   B. being held up   C. having held up   D. to hold up

19. It is always interesting _____ people in airports while you're waiting for a flight.
    A. being observed
    B. observe
    C. to have observed
    D. to observe

20. I got everyone in the family _____ Jane's birthday card before I sent it to her.
    A. sign   B. signed   C. to sign   D. having signed

◇ **PRACTICE 15. Verb form review. (Charts 14-1 → 15-9)**
   Directions: Complete each sentence with an appropriate form of the verb in parentheses.

1. Bill decided *(buy)* ___to buy___ a new car rather than a used one.

2. We delayed *(open)* _____ the doors of the examination room until exactly 9:00.

3. I really dislike *(ask)* _____ to answer questions in class when I haven't prepared my lesson.

4. I certainly didn't anticipate *(have)* _____ to wait in line for three hours for tickets to the baseball game!

5. When I was younger, I used *(wear)* _____ mini-skirts and bright colors. Now I am accustomed to *(dress)* _____ more conservatively.

6. Skydivers must have nerves of steel. I can't imagine *(jump)* _____ out of a plane and *(fall)* _____ to the earth. What if the parachute didn't open?

7. We are looking forward to *(take)* _____ on a tour of Athens by our Greek friends.

8. I told the mail carrier that we would be away for two weeks on vacation. I asked her *(stop)* _____ *(deliver)* _____ our mail until the 21st. She told me *(fill)* _____ out a form at the post office so that the post office would hold our mail until we returned.

9. The elderly man next door is just sitting in his rocking chair *(gaze)* _____ out the window. I wish there were something I could do *(cheer)* _____ him up.

10. I resent *(have)* _____ to work on this project with Fred. I know I'll end up with most of the work falling on my shoulders.

11. Rick moved from a big city to a small town. He appreciates *(be)* _____ able to drive to work in five minutes with very little traffic congestion.

12. The power lines outside my house were dangerous. I finally got the power company *(move)* _____ them to a safer place.

13. I wanted *(help)* _____ them *(resolve)* _____ their differences, but Sally persuaded me *(interfere, not)* _____ .

14. Sara was encouraged by her teachers *(apply)* _____ for study at the Art Institute.

15. I was happy *(learn)* _____ of your new position in the company, but I was disappointed *(discover)* _____ that you had recommended *(promote)* _____ Carl to your old position instead of me.

16. I don't mind *(remind)* _____ you every day *(lock)* _____ the door when you leave the apartment, but I would appreciate your *(try)* _____ *(remember)* _____ on your own.

17. Now I remember your *(ask)* _____ me to bring sandwiches to the picnic. Your complaints about my *(forget)* _____ things seem justified. I'm sorry.

18. After our automobile accident, the insurance company had a stack of papers for us to sign, but our lawyer advised us *(sign, not)* _____ them until she had a chance to study them very carefully.

19. John was responsible for *(notify)* _____ everyone about the meeting, but he apparently failed *(call)* _____ several people. As a result, not enough people showed up, and we have to try to get everybody together again soon.

20. You shouldn't let children *(play)* _____ with matches.

21. Art smelled something *(burn)* _____ . When he ran into the kitchen, he saw

 fire *(come)* _____ out of the oven and panicked. If Barbara hadn't come

 running in with the fire extinguisher, I don't know what would have happened.

22. I finally told him *(be)* _____ quiet for a minute and *(listen)* _____ to

 what I had to say.

23. Irene was lying in bed *(think)* _____ about what a wonderful time she'd had.

24. The illogic of his statements made me *(tear)* _____ my hair out.

25. Recently Jo has been spending most of her time *(do)* _____ research for a book on

 pioneer women.

26. Mary Beth suggested *(go)* _____ on a picnic.

27. Isabel expected *(admit)* _____ to the university, but she wasn't.

28. Jason wouldn't let them *(take)* _____ his picture.

29. I couldn't understand what the passage said, so I had my friend *(translate)* _____

 it for me.

30. No, that's not what I meant *(say)* _____ . How can I make you *(understand)*

 _____ ?

31. I have finally assembled enough information *(begin)* _____ writing my thesis.

32. It's a serious problem. Something needs *(do)* _____ about it soon.

33. I was terribly disappointed *(discover)* _____ that he had lied to me.

34. I had the operator (put) _____ the call through for me.

35. No one could make Ted (feel) _____ afraid. He refused (intimidate) _____ _____ by anyone.

36. I don't see how she can possibly avoid (fail) _____ the course.

37. Do something! Don't just sit there (twiddle) _____ your thumbs.

38. I don't know how to get to Harry's house, so I had him (draw) _____ a map for me.

39. Barbara has a wonderful sense of humor. She can always make me (laugh) _____ .

40. The teacher had the class (open) _____ their books to page 185.

41. I found my roommate in the other room (sleep) _____ on the floor in the middle of the day.

42. They refused (pay) _____ their taxes, so they were sent to jail.

43. I admit (be) _____ a little nervous about the job interview. I don't know what (expect) _____ .

44. I found a coin (lie) _____ on the sidewalk.

◇ **PRACTICE 16. Verb form review. (Charts 14-1 → 15-9)**
   Directions: Complete each sentence with an appropriate form of the verb in parentheses.

1. After I decided (have) _____ a garage (build) _____ next to the house, I hired a carpenter (do) _____ the work.

2. The coach didn't let anyone (watch) _____ the team (practice) _____ before the championship game. He wanted to keep the opposing team from (find) _____ out about the new plays he had devised.

3. My son is playing in his first piano recital this evening. I'm looking forward to (hear) _____ him (play) _____ , but I know he's worried about (forget) _____ the right notes and (make) _____ a fool of himself. I told him just (relax) _____ and (enjoy) _____ himself.

4. There's not much point in (waste) _____ a lot of time and energy on that project. It's likely (fail) _____ no matter what we do. Spend your time (do) _____ something more worthwhile.

5. (Attend) _____ the dance proved to be an (embarrass) _____

experience for me, especially since I don't know how to dance. I felt like a fish out of water. I

wanted (hide) _____ someplace or (get) _____ out of there, but

my friend wouldn't let me (leave) _____.

6. I'm over sixty now, but I enjoy (recall) _____ my high-school days. I

remember (choose) _____ by my classmates as "Most Likely to

Succeed" when I was a senior. My best friend was chosen as "Least Likely to Succeed," and

he is now the president of an electronics company. Once in a while when we get together,

we have a good time (look) _____ through the high-school yearbook and

(laugh) _____ at the way we looked then. We reminisce about (act)

_____ in school dramas and (play) _____ on the basketball

team. We remember (be) _____ serious young men who knew how to have

fun. We congratulate ourselves for (achieve) _____ more than we had

thought we could when we were eighteen.

7. Our house needs (clean) _____. The floors need (sweep)

_____. The dishes need (wash) _____.

The furniture needs (dust) _____. However, I think I'll read a

book. (Read) _____ is a lot more interesting than (do) _____

housework.

8. As an adult, I very much appreciate (give) _____ the opportunity

to travel extensively with my parents when I was a child. Those experiences were important

in (form) _____ my view of the world. I learned (accept) _____

different customs and beliefs. At times, I would resist (go) _____ away on another

trip, especially when I was a teenager. In the end, I always accompanied my parents, and I

am grateful that I did. I didn't understand at that time how those trips would influence my

later life. My (be) _____ a compassionate and caring adult is due in large part to

my (expose) _____ to many different ways of life as a child.

9. (Find) _____ a cure for the common cold does not appear (be) _____

imminent. Colds are caused by hundreds of different viruses. You can possibly avoid

(expose) _____ to the viruses by (stay) _____ away

from those with colds, but it's almost impossible (avoid) _____ the viruses completely. If you want *(minimize)* _____ the risk of *(get)* _____ a cold, it is prudent *(get)* _____ enough rest and *(eat)* _____ properly. Some people believe in *(take)* _____ large amounts of Vitamin C. In the long run, it is probably easier *(prevent)* _____ *(catch)* _____ a cold than it is to cure one.

10. Modern cars have systems that protect us from *(inconvenience)* _____ _____ or *(hurt)* _____ by our own carelessness. In most cars, when the keys are left in the ignition, a buzz sounds in order *(remind)* _____ the driver *(remove)* _____ them. In some models, if the driver does not remember *(turn)* _____ off the lights, it does not matter because the lights go off automatically. In some cases, when the seat belts are not buckled, the ignition does not start, and then the driver is actually forced *(buckle)* _____ up. Often when the driver has failed *(shut)* _____ a door properly, another signal noise may be given. A few cars emit sounds to warn us *(fill)* _____ the tank before it is completely empty.

It is easy *(forget)* _____ *(do)* _____ many routine tasks in *(drive)* _____ a car. The automatic warning systems help drivers *(avoid)* _____ *(make)* _____ some common mistakes. While some people may resent *(instruct)* _____ by their own automobiles *(perform)* _____ certain procedures, many others do not mind at all *(remind)* _____ *(carry)* _____ out these easily overlooked procedures.

◇ **PRACTICE 17. TEST A: Gerunds and infinitives.** (Chapters 14 and 15)
   Directions: Choose the correct answer.

Example: The office staff decided ___C___ a retirement party for Dolores.
   A. having had   B. to have had   C. to have   D. having

1. I don't blame you for not _____ outside in this awful weather.
   A. wanting to go   B. wanting go   C. want to go   D. to want go

2. I think I hear someone _____ the back window. Do you hear it, too?
   A. trying open   B. trying to open   C. try opening   D. try to open

3. When Alan was questioned by the police, he admitted knowing about the embezzlement of
   funds from his company, but denied _____ in any way.
   A. to be involved   B. involving   C. having involved   D. being involved

4. Mr. Lee was upset by _____ him the truth.
   A. our not having told   C. we didn't tell
   B. us not tell   D. not to tell

5. We considered _____ after work.
   A. to go shop   B. going shopping   C. going to shop   D. to go to shop

6. Jack offered _____ care of my garden while I was out of town.
   A. take   B. taking   C. to have taken   D. to take

7. Could you please come over? I need you _____ the refrigerator.
   A. help me moving   C. to help me move
   B. helping me to move   D. help me to move

8. I just heard that there's been a major accident that has all of the traffic tied up. If we want
   to get to the play on time, we'd better avoid _____ the highway.
   A. having taken   B. take   C. to take   D. taking

9. The painting was beautiful. I stood there _____ it for a long time.
   A. for admiring   B. being admired   C. admire   D. admiring

10. Jim should have asked for help instead _____ to do it himself.
    A. of trying   B. to try   C. try   D. from trying

11. A plane with an engine on fire approached the runway. _____ was frightening. There
    could have been a terrible accident.
    A. Watch it landing   C. To watch it land
    B. Watching it land   D. Watching to land it

12. The customs officer opened the suitcase _____ if anything illegal was being brought into
    the country.
    A. seeing   B. for seeing   C. see   D. to see

13. Sometimes very young children have trouble _____ fact from fiction and may believe that
    dragons actually exist.
    A. to separate   B. separating   C. to be separated   D. for separating

14. Do you have an excuse _____ late to class two days in a row?
    A. for to be   B. for being   C. to be   D. being

15. Jack made me _____ him next week.
    A. to promise to call   C. promise to call
    B. to promise calling   D. promise calling

16. I got Barbara _____ her car for the weekend.
    A. to let me to borrow   C. to let me borrow
    B. let me borrow   D. let me to borrow

17. I'll never forget _____ that race. What a thrill!
    A. to win   B. win   C. being won   D. winning

18. No one has better qualifications. Carol is certain _____ for the job.
    A. to choose   B. having chosen   C. to be chosen   D. being chosen

19. I was enjoying my book, but I stopped _____ a program on TV.
    A. reading to watch   C. to read for watching
    B. to read to watch   D. reading for to watch

20. Who is the woman talking to Mr. Quinn? I don't recall _____ her around the office before.
    A. to have seen   B. seeing   C. to see   D. being seen

◇ **PRACTICE 18. TEST B: Gerunds and infinitives. (Chapters 14 and 15)**
Directions: Choose the correct answer.

Example: The office staff decided ___C___ a retirement party for Dolores.
    A. having had   B. to have had   C. to have   D. having

1. Roger proved that the accident wasn't his fault by _____ two witnesses who testified in his favor.
    A. produce   B. produced   C. to produce   D. producing

2. The front door is warped from the humidity. We have a difficult time _____ it.
    A. open   B. to open   C. having opened   D. opening

3. I stood up at the meeting and demanded _____. At last, I got the chance to express my opinion.
    A. to be heard   C. having been heard
    B. to hear   D. to have heard

4. Did you ever finish _____ the office for that new client of yours?
    A. to design   B. designing   C. designed   D. having designed

5. It's a beautiful day, and I have my brother's boat. Would you like to go _____?
    A. to sail   B. sailing   C. to sailing   D. for sailing

6. I called a plumber _____ the kitchen sink.
    A. for repairing   B. for to repair   C. to repair   D. to be repaired

7. I'm angry because you didn't tell me the truth. I don't like _____.
    A. deceiving   B. to deceive   C. being deceived   D. having deceived

8. A good teacher makes her students _____ the world from new perspectives.
    A. to view   B. viewing   C. view   D. to be viewed

9. Please remember _____ your hand during the test if you have a question.
    A. raising   B. to raise   C. having raised   D. to have raised

10. It is important _____ care of your health.
    A. to take   B. to be taken   C. take   D. taken

11. _____ in restaurants as often as they do is very expensive.
    A. Being eaten   C. Having been eating
    B. Having eaten   D. Eating

12. I expect Mary _____ here early tonight. She should arrive in the next half hour.
    A. to come   B. coming   C. having come   D. to have come

13. I advised my niece not _____ at an early age.
    A. marrying   C. to marry
    B. being married   D. to have been married

14. Shhh! I hear someone _____ in the distance. Do you hear it, too?
    A. shout   B. shouted   C. to shout   D. shouting

15. I don't understand _____ your job so suddenly. Why did you do that?
   A. your quitting
   B. you to have quit
   C. to quit
   D. you quit

16. Last night, we saw a meteor _____ through the sky.
   A. streaked   B. to streak   C. streak   D. to have streaked

17. My parents wouldn't let me _____ up late when I was a child.
   A. to be stay   B. staying   C. to stay   D. stay

18. Children should be encouraged _____ their individual interests.
   A. develop   B. to be developed   C. to develop   D. developing

19. This room is too dark. We need _____ a lighter shade.
   A. to have it painted
   B. to be painted
   C. painting it
   D. to have it paint

20. I'm sorry I never graduated. I've always regretted not _____ college.
   A. to finish   B. finish   C. finished   D. having finished

CHAPTER 16
Coordinating Conjunctions

◇ **PRACTICE 1. Parallel structure. (Chart 16-1)**

Directions: Write the words that are parallel in each of the sentences.

1. These apples are fresh and sweet.
   1. ___fresh___ and ___sweet___
      (adjective) + (adjective)

2. These apples and pears are fresh.
   2. _____ and _____
      (noun) + (noun)

3. I washed and dried the apples.
   3. _____ and _____
      (verb) + (verb)

4. I am washing and drying the apples.
   4. _____ and _____
      (verb) + (verb)

5. We ate the fruit happily and quickly.
   5. _____ and _____
      (adverb) + (adverb)

6. I enjoy biting into a fresh apple and tasting the juicy sweetness.
   6. _____ and _____
      (gerund) + (gerund)

7. I like to bite into a fresh apple and taste the juicy sweetness.
   7. _____ and _____
      (infinitive) + (infinitive)

8. Those imported apples are delicious but expensive.
   8. _____ but _____
      (adjective) + (adjective)

9. Apples, pears, and bananas are kinds of fruit.
   9. _____, _____, and _____
      (noun) (noun) + (noun)

10. Those apples are red, ripe, and juicy.
   10. _____, _____, and _____
      (adjective) (adjective) + (adjective)

◇ **PRACTICE 2. Parallel structure: use of commas. (Chart 16-1)**

Directions: Add commas as appropriate.

1. Jack was calm and quiet. *(no commas)*
2. Jack was calm quiet and serene.
   → *Jack was calm, quiet,* and serene.*

---

*The comma before *and* in a series is optional. See Chart 16-1.

3. The children sang and danced.

4. The children sang danced and played games.

5. Tom and Tariq joined the soccer game.

6. Tom Tariq and Francisco joined the soccer game.

7. I told the children to sit down be quiet and open their reading books.

8. I told the children to sit down and be quiet.

9. Did you know that the pupil* of your eye expands and contracts slightly with each heartbeat?

10. Our waitress's tray held two cups of coffee three glasses of water and one glass of orange juice.

11. My parents were strict but fair with their children.

12. Is a newborn blue whale smaller or larger than an adult elephant?

◇ **PRACTICE 3. Parallel structure. (Charts 16-1 and 16-2)**
   Directions: Write "**C**" if the parallel structure is CORRECT. Write "**I**" if the parallel structure is INCORRECT, and make any necessary corrections. <u>Underline</u> the parallel elements of the sentences.

1. ___I___ I admire him for his <u>intelligence</u>, cheerful <u>disposition</u>, and ~~he is honest~~. honesty

2. ___C___ Abraham Lincoln was a <u>lawyer</u> and a <u>politician</u>.

3. _____ The boat sailed across the lake smoothly and quiet.

4. _____ Barb studies each problem carefully and works out a solution.

5. _____ Aluminum is plentiful and relatively inexpensive.

6. _____ Many visitors to Los Angeles enjoy visiting Disneyland and to tour movie studios.

7. _____ Children are usually interested in but a little frightened by snakes.

8. _____ Either fainting can result from a lack of oxygen or a loss of blood.

9. _____ So far this term, the students in the writing class have learned how to write thesis statements, organize their material, and summarizing their conclusions.

10. _____ When I looked more closely, I saw that it was not coffee but chocolate on my necktie.

11. _____ Not only universities support medical research but also many government agencies.

12. _____ Physics explains why water freezes and how the sun produces heat.

13. _____ All plants need light, a suitable climate, and an ample supply of water and minerals from the soil.

14. _____ With their keen sight, fine hearing, and refined sense of smell, wolves hunt day or night in quest of elk, deer, moose, or caribou.

---

*The pupil of one's eye is the dark center of the eye.

15. _____ The comedian made people laugh by telling jokes and make funny faces.

16. _____ Tina is always understanding, patient, and sensitive when helping her friends with their problems.

17. _____ Not only the post office but also all banks close on national holidays.

18. _____ Walking briskly for 30 minutes or to run for 15 minutes will burn an approximately equal number of calories.

◇ **PRACTICE 4. Parallel structure. (Chart 16-1)**
Directions: Choose the letter of the phrase from the list that best completes each sentence.
Use each phrase in the list only once.

A. reliable health care	E. provide quality education
B. carefully	F. responsible
C. excellence in	G. seeking practical solutions
✔ D. in agriculture	H. who finds a way to get the important jobs done

1. Mr. Turner has had wide experience. He has worked in business, in the news media, and ___D___ .

2. People want safe homes, good schools, and _____ .

3. As a taxpayer, I want my money used wisely and _____ .

4. Mrs. Adams is respected for researching issues and _____ .

5. Ms. Hunter has established a record of effective and _____ leadership in government.

6. She has worked hard to control excess government spending, protect our environment, and _____ .

7. Carol is a hard-working personnel manager who welcomes challenges and _____ .

8. I will continue to fight for adequate funding of and _____ education.

◇ **PRACTICE 5. Paired conjunctions: subject–verb agreement. (Chart 16-2)**
Directions: Supply the correct present tense form of the verb in parentheses.

1. *(know)* Neither the students nor the teacher ___knows___ the answer.

2. *(know)* Neither the teacher nor the students ___know___ the answer.

3. *(know)* Not only the students but also the teacher _____ the answer.

4. *(know)* Not only the teacher but also the students _____ the answer.

5. *(know)* Both the teacher and the students _____ the answer.

6. *(want)* Neither Alan nor Carol _____ to go skiing this weekend.

7. *(like)* Both John and Ted _____ to go cross-country skiing.

8. *(have)* Either Jack or Alice _____ the information you need.

9. *(agree)* Neither my parents nor my brother _____ with my decision.

10. *(be)*   Both intelligence and skill _____ essential to good teaching.

11. *(realize)* Neither my classmates nor my teacher _____ that I have no idea what's going on in class.

12. *(think)*   Not only Laura's husband but also her children _____ she should return to school and finish her graduate degree.

◇ **PRACTICE 6. Paired conjunctions. (Chart 16-2)**
Directions: Combine the following into sentences which contain parallel structure. Use the paired conjunctions in parentheses. Pay special attention to the exact place you put the paired conjunctions in the combined sentence.

1. Many people don't drink coffee. Many people don't drink alcohol. *(neither . . . nor)*
   → *Many people drink neither coffee nor alcohol.*

2. Barbara is fluent in Chinese. She is also fluent in Japanese. *(not only . . . but also)*

3. I'm sorry to say that Paul has no patience. He has no sensitivity to others. *(neither . . . nor)*

4. She can sing. She can dance. *(both . . . and)*

5. If you want to change your class schedule, you should talk to your teacher, or you should talk to your academic counselor. *(either . . . or)*

6. Diana is intelligent. She is very creative. *(both . . . and)*

7. You may begin working tomorrow or you may begin next week. *(either . . . or)*

8. Michael didn't tell his mother about the trouble he had gotten into. He didn't tell his father about the trouble he had gotten into. *(neither . . . nor)*

9. Success in karate requires balance and skill. Success in karate requires concentration and mental alertness. *(not only . . . but also)*

◇ **PRACTICE 7. Combining independent clauses: periods and commas.**
(Charts 16-1 and 16-3)

Directions: Punctuate these sentences by adding periods (.) or commas (,) as necessary. Do not add any words. Capitalize letters where necessary. Some sentences need no changes.

1. I like French cooking my wife prefers Italian cooking.
   → *I like French cooking. My wife prefers Italian cooking.*

2. I like French cooking but my wife prefers Italian cooking.
   → *I like French cooking, but my wife prefers Italian cooking. (optional comma)*

3. I've read that book it's very good.

4. I've read that book but I didn't like it.

5. I opened the door and asked my friend to come in.

6. I opened the door my sister answered the phone.

7. I opened the door and my sister answered the phone.

8. Minerals are common materials they are found in rocks and soil.

9. The most common solid materials on earth are minerals they are found in rocks soil and water.

10. You can travel to England by plane or you can go by ship if you prefer.

11. You can travel to England by plane or by ship.

12. Jason was going to study all night so he declined our invitation to dinner.

13. Jason declined our invitation to dinner he needed to stay home and study.

14. The wind was howling outside yet it was warm and comfortable indoors.

15. I hurried to answer the phone for I didn't want the children to wake up.

16. Last weekend we went camping it rained the entire time.

17. The highway was under construction so we had to take a different route to work.

18. No one thought we would win the championship yet our team won by a large margin.

19. We arrived at the theater late but the play had not yet begun we were quite surprised.

20. A central heating system provides heat for an entire building from one central place most central heating systems service only one building but some systems heat a group of buildings, such as those at a military base a campus or an apartment complex.

◇ **PRACTICE 8. Combining independent clauses: periods and commas.**
(Charts 16-1 and 16-3)

Directions: Find and correct the errors in punctuation and capitalization.

I spent yesterday with my brother. **W**we had a really good time he's visiting me for a couple of days so I decided not to go to work yesterday we spent the day in the city first I took him to the waterfront we went to the aquarium, where we saw fearsome sharks some wonderfully funny marine mammals and all kinds of tropical fish after the aquarium, we went downtown to a big mall and went shopping my brother doesn't like to shop as much as I do so we didn't stay there long.

I had trouble thinking of a place to take him for lunch for he's a strict vegetarian luckily I finally remembered a restaurant that has vegan food so we went there and had a wonderful lunch of fresh vegetables and whole grains I'm not a vegetarian yet I must say that I really enjoyed the meal.

In the afternoon it started raining so we went to a movie it was pretty good but had too much violence for me I felt tense when we left the theater I prefer comedies or dramas my brother loved the movie.

We ended the day with a good home-cooked meal and some good talk in my living room it was a good day I like spending time with my brother.

◇ **PRACTICE 9. Combining independent clauses: periods and commas. (Charts 16-1 and 16-3)**

Directions: Find and correct the errors in punctuation and capitalization.

Some of the most interesting working women of the American West in the nineteenth century were African-American women Mary Fields was one of them she had been born a slave in the mid-1800s in the South but moved west to the Rocky Mountains as a free woman in 1884 her first job was hauling freight she drove a wagon and delivered freight in the valleys and mountains of Montana she was tall strong and fast on the draw* she didn't hesitate to protect her wagon of goods with her gun.

She drove a freight wagon for many years then in her late fifties she opened a restaurant but her business failed so in her sixties she became a stagecoach driver carrying the U.S. mail because of outlaws, driving a mailcoach was dangerous yet her mailcoach always arrived safely in her seventies she opened her own laundry business she continued successfully in that business until her death in 1914.

Mary Fields deserves our respect and can be seen as a role model by young women everywhere for she rose above unfortunate circumstances and became a determined hardworking and successful businesswoman

---

*"Fast on the draw" means that she could pull her gun out of her belt or holster and shoot fast.

CHAPTER 17
Adverb Clauses

◇ **PRACTICE 1. Adverb Clauses. (Chart 17-1)**

Directions: Change the position of the adverb clause in the sentence. Underline the adverb clause in the given sentence, and underline the adverb clause in the new sentence. Punctuate carefully.

Example: Sue dropped a carton of eggs <u>as she was leaving the store</u>.
→ <u>*As Sue was leaving the store*</u>**,** *she dropped a carton of eggs.* ★

1. We'll all take a walk in the park after Dad finishes working on the car.

2. Since Douglas fell off his bicycle last week, he has had to use crutches to walk.

3. Because I already had my boarding pass, I didn't have to stand in line at the airline counter.

4. Productivity in a factory increases if the workplace is made pleasant.

5. After Ceylon had been independent for 24 years, the country's name was changed to Sri Lanka.

6. Ms. Johnson regularly returns her e-mail messages as soon as she has some free time from her principal duties.

7. Tarik will be able to work more efficiently once he becomes familiar with the new computer program.

8. When the flooding river raced down the valley, it destroyed everything in its path.

◇ **PRACTICE 2. Periods and commas. (Charts 16-1, 16-3, and 17-1)**

Directions: Add periods and commas as necessary. Do not change, add, or omit any words. Capitalize as necessary.

1. The lake was calm Tom went fishing.
   → *The lake was calm. Tom went fishing.*

2. Because the lake was calm Tom went fishing.
   → *Because the lake was calm, Tom went fishing.*

---

*★Also possible: **As she was leaving the store,** Sue dropped a carton of eggs.*

3. Tom went fishing because the lake was calm he caught two fish.

4. Tom went fishing because the lake was calm and caught two fish.

5. When Tom went fishing the lake was calm he caught two fish.

6. The lake was calm so Tom went fishing he caught two fish.

7. Because the lake was calm and quiet Tom went fishing.

8. The lake was calm quiet and clear when Tom went fishing.

9. Mr. Hood is admired because he dedicated his life to helping the poor he is well known for his work on behalf of homeless people.

10. Microscopes automobile dashboards and cameras are awkward for left-handed people to use they are designed for right-handed people when "lefties" use these items they have to use their right hand to do the things that they would normally do with their left hand.

◇ **PRACTICE 3. Verb tenses in adverb clauses of time. (Chapter 5 and Chart 17-1)**
Directions: Choose the letter of the correct answer.

1. After Marco __C__ his degree, he plans to seek employment in an engineering firm.
   A. will finish   C. finishes
   B. will have finished   D. is finishing

2. By the time Colette leaves work today, she _____ the budget report.
   A. will finish   B. has finished   C. will have finished   D. finishes

3. When my aunt _____ into the airport tomorrow, I'll be at work, so I can't pick her up.
   A. will get   B. got   C. will have gotten   D. gets

4. Natasha heard a small "meow" and looked down to discover a kitten at her feet. When she saw it, she _____.
   A. was smiling   B. had smiled   C. smiled   D. smiles

5. Ahmed has trouble keeping a job. By the time Ahmed was thirty, he _____ eight different jobs.
   A. had   B. was having   C. had had   D. had been having

6. Maria waits until her husband Al _____ to work before she calls her friends on the phone.
   A. will go   B. went   C. will have gone   D. goes

7. I went to an opera at Lincoln Center the last time I _____ to New York City.
   A. go   B. went   C. had gone   D. have gone

8. When the police arrived, the building was empty. The thieves _____ and escaped through an unlocked window.
   A. will have entered   C. have entered
   B. had entered   D. entered

9. It seems that whenever I try to take some quiet time for myself, the phone _____.
   A. has been ringing   C. rings
   B. is ringing   D. has rung

10. I'll invite the Thompsons to the potluck the next time I _____ them.
    A. see   B. will see   C. will have seen   D. have seen

11. I _____ hard to help support my family ever since I was a child.
    A. worked   B. work   C. am working   D. have worked

12. A small animal ran across the path in front of me as I _____ through the woods.
    A. was walking   B. had walked   C. am walking   D. had been walking

◇ **PRACTICE 4. Using adverb clauses to show cause-and-effect relationships. (Chart 17-2)**
Directions: Combine the sentences, using the word or phrase in parentheses. Add commas where necessary. Make two sentences for each, showing the two possible positions of the adverb clause. <u>Underline</u> the adverb clause.

Example: Our flight was delayed. We decided to take a long walk around the terminal. *(since)*
   → *<u>Since our flight was delayed</u>, we decided to take a long walk around the terminal.*
   → *We decided to take a long walk around the terminal <u>since our flight was delayed</u>.*

1. My registration was canceled. I didn't pay my fees on time. *(because)*

2. Erica has qualified for the Olympics in speedskating. She must train even more vigorously. *(now that)*

3. We decided not to buy the house on Fourth Street. It's directly below flight patterns from the nearby international airport. *(since)*

◇ **PRACTICE 5. Using *even though* vs. *because*. (Charts 17-2 and 17-3)**
Directions: Complete the sentences with *even though* or *because*.

1. I put on my raincoat ___*even though*___ it was a bright, sunny day.

2. I put on my raincoat ___*because*___ it was raining.

3. _____ Sue is a good student, she received a scholarship.

4 _____ Ann is a good student, she didn't receive a scholarship.

5. _____ it was raining, we went for a walk.

6. _____ it was raining, we didn't go for a walk.

7. This letter was delivered _____ it didn't have enough postage.

8. That letter was returned to the sender _____ it didn't have enough postage.

9. I'm going horseback riding with Judy this afternoon _____ I'm afraid of horses.

10. I'm going horseback riding with Judy this afternoon _____ I enjoy it.

11. _____ you've made it clear that you don't want any help, I have to at least offer to help you.

12. I knew that I should get some sleep, but I just couldn't put my book down _____ I was really enjoying it.

13. _____ Tom didn't know how to dance, he wanted to go to the school dance _____ he felt lonely sitting at home and staring blankly at the TV while all of his friends were having fun together.

14. My hair stylist subscribes to three different fashion magazines _____ she's not interested in clothes. She subscribes to them _____ her customers like them.

◇ PRACTICE 6. Direct contrast: *while* and *whereas*. (Chart 17-4)
Directions: Write "**C**" if the sentence (including punctuation) is CORRECT. Write "**I**" if the sentence is INCORRECT.

1. __*C*__ While some chairs are soft, others are hard.

2. _____ While some chairs are hard, others are soft.

3. _____ Some chairs are soft, while others are hard.

4. _____ Some chairs are hard, while others are soft.

5. _____ Whereas some chairs are soft, others are hard.

6. _____ Some chairs are hard, whereas others are soft.

7. _____ Some chairs are soft, whereas others are hard.

8. _____ Whereas some chairs are hard, others are soft.

9. _____ While some chairs are soft, others are comfortable.

◇ PRACTICE 7. *If*-clauses. (Chart 17-5)
Directions: Underline the *if*-clause. Correct any errors in verb forms.

1. Let's not go to the park if it ~~will rain~~ *rains* tomorrow.

2. <u>If my car doesn't start tomorrow morning</u>, I'll take the bus to work. *(no change)*

3. If I have free time during my work day, I send e-mail messages to friends.

4. I'll send you an e-mail if I will have some free time tomorrow.

5. If we don't leave within the next ten minutes, we are late to the theater.

6. If we will leave within the next two minutes, we will make it to the theater on time.

◇ PRACTICE 8. Using *whether or not* and *even if*. (Chart 17-6)
Directions: Complete the sentences, using the given information.

1. Tom is going to go to the horse races no matter what. He doesn't care if his wife approves.

   In other words, Tom is going to go to the horse races even if his wife __*doesn't approve*__.

   He's going to go whether his wife __*approves*__ or not.

2. Fatima is determined to buy an expensive car. It doesn't matter to her if she can't afford it. In other words, Fatima is going to buy an expensive car whether she _____ _____ it or not. She's going to buy one even if she _____ it.

3. William wears his raincoat every day. He wears it when it's raining. He wears it when it's not raining. In other words, William wears his raincoat whether it _____ or not. He wears it even if it _____ .

4. Some students don't understand what the teacher is saying, but still they smile and nod. In other words, even if they _____ what the teacher is saying, they smile and nod. They smile and nod whether they _____ what the teacher is saying or not.

◇ **PRACTICE 9. Using *in case* and *in the event that*. (Chart 17-7)**
   Directions: Complete the sentences by using *in case*. Decide if it goes in the first blank or in the second blank. Add necessary punctuation and capitalization.

   PART I.

   1. ___In case___ you need to get in touch with me**,** I'll be in my office until late this evening.

   2. _W_ ~~w~~e'll be at the Swan Hotel ___in case___ you need to call us.

   3. Mary is willing to work with you on your design project. _____ you find that you need help with it _____ she'll be back in town next Monday and can meet with you then.

   4 _____ my boss has to stay near a phone all weekend _____ the company wants him to go to London to close the deal they've been working on all month.

   5. _____ I'm not back in time to make dinner _____ I put the phone number for carry-out Chinese food on the refrigerator. You can call and order the food for yourself.

   PART II. Complete the sentences using *in the event that*.

   6. ___In the event that___ Janet is late for work again tomorrow**,** she will be fired.

   7. Are you sure you're taking enough money with you? _____ you'd better take a credit card with you _____ you run out of cash.

   8. The political situation is getting more unstable and dangerous. _____ my family plans to leave the country _____ there is civil war.

   9. Just to be on the safe side, _____ I always take a change of clothes in my carry-on bag _____ the airline loses my luggage.

   10. Ann is one of five people nominated for an award to be given at the banquet this evening. _____ she has already prepared an acceptance speech _____ _____ she wins it tonight.

◇ **PRACTICE 10. Using _unless_ vs. _if_ and _only if_. (Charts 17-8 and 17-9)**
   Directions: Choose the correct answer.

1. I'll give you a hand ___B___ you need it, but I hope I don't hurt my back.
   A. unless   B. if

2. I can't buy a car _____ I save enough money.
   A. unless   B. only if

3. Our kids are allowed to watch television after dinner _____ they have finished their homework. Homework must come first.
   A. unless   B. only if

4. There can be peace in the world _____ all nations sincerely lend their energy to that effort.
   A. unless   B. only if

5. I'm afraid the battery is dead. _____ I buy a new one, the car won't start.
   A. Unless   B. If

6. Let's plan on an old-fashioned sit-down dinner with the whole family at the table at once. I'll prepare a really special dinner _____ you all promise to be home on time this evening.
   A. unless   B. only if

◇ **PRACTICE 11. Adverb clauses of condition. (Charts 17-5 → 17-9)**
   Directions: Choose the correct words in *italics* so that the sentences make sense.

1. I'll pass the course only if I (*pass,*) *don't pass* the final examination.

2. I'm *going to go, not going to go* to the park unless the weather is nice.

3. I'm going to the park unless it *rains, doesn't rain.*

4. Tom doesn't like to work. He'll get a job *unless, only if* he has to.

5. I *always eat, never eat* breakfast unless I get up late and don't have enough time.

6. I always finish my homework *even if, only if* I'm sleepy and want to go to bed.

7. You *will, won't* learn to play the violin well unless you practice every day.

8. Even if the president calls, *wake, don't wake* me up. I don't want to talk to anyone. I want to sleep.

9. Jack is going to come to the game with us today *if, unless* his boss gives him the afternoon off.

10. *Borrow, Don't borrow* money from your friends unless you absolutely must.

◇ **PRACTICE 12. Using *only if* vs. *if*: subject–verb inversion. (Chart 17-9)**
   Directions: Change the position of the adverb clause to the front of the sentence. Make any necessary changes in the verb of the main clause.

   1. I can finish this work on time only if you help me.
      → ***Only if** you help me **can I finish** this work on time.*

   2. I can finish this work on time if you help me.
      → ***If** you help me, **I can finish** this work on time.*

   3. I will go only if I am invited.

   4. I will go if I am invited.

   5. I eat only if I am hungry.

   6. I usually eat some fruit if I am hungry during the morning.

   7. You will be considered for that job only if you know both Arabic and Spanish.

   8. John goes to the market only if the refrigerator is empty.

   9. I will tell you the truth about what happened only if you promise not to get angry.

   10. I won't marry you if you can't learn to communicate your feelings.

◇ **PRACTICE 13. Summary: abverb clauses. (Chapter 17)**
   Directions: Choose the best completion.

   1. Alice will tutor you in math _____ you promise to do everything she says.
      A. unless   B. only if   C. whereas   D. even though

   2. Oscar won't pass his math course _____ he gets a tutor.
      A. because   B. in the event that   C. unless   D. only if

   3. Most people you meet will be polite to you _____ you are polite to them.
      A. in case   B. only if   C. unless   D. if

   4. I'm glad that my mother made me take piano lessons when I was a child _____ I hated it at the time. Now, I play the piano every day.
      A. even though   B. because   C. unless   D. if

   5. Chicken eggs will not hatch _____ they are kept at the proper temperature.
      A. because   B. unless   C. only if   D. even though

   6. You'd better take your raincoat with you _____ the weather changes. It could rain before you get home again.
      A. now that   B. even if   C. in case   D. only if

7. Ms. Jackson was assigned the fifth-grade science class _____ she has the best qualifications among the available faculty.

    A. although   B. whereas   C. if   D. since

8. My sister can fall asleep under any conditions, but I can't get to sleep _____ the light is off and the room is perfectly quiet.

    A. if   B. unless   C. in case   D. now that

9. The majority will of the people rules in a democracy, _____ in a dictatorship, power is in the hands of a single person.

    A. because   B. even though   C. while   D. unless

10. The cheapest way to get from an airport to a hotel is to take an airport bus, but I'm not sure if River City has one. _____ there is no airport bus, you can always take a taxi.

    A. Unless   B. Now that   C. In the event that   D. Even though

11. _____ my country has a new democractic government, the people at last have more freedom.

    A. Even though   B. Even if   C. In the event that   D. Now that

12. Parents love and support their children _____ the children misbehave or do foolish things.

    A. even if   B. since   C. if   D. only if

CHAPTER 18
Reduction of Adverb Clauses to Modifying Adverbial Phrases

◇ **PRACTICE 1. Reduction of adverb clauses to modifying phrases. (Charts 18-1 → 18-3)**
Directions: Change the adverb clause to a modifying phrase.

> *opening*
1. Since ~~he opened~~ his new business, Bob has been working 16 hours a day.

2. I shut off the lights before I left the room

3. While he was herding his goats in the mountains, an Ethiopian named Kaldi discovered the coffee plant more than 1200 years ago.

4. Before they marched into battle, ancient Ethiopian soldiers ate a mixture of raw coffee beans and fat for extra energy.

5. After I had met the movie star in person, I understood why she was so popular.

6. I found my keys after I searched through all my pockets.

7. When it was first brought to Europe, the tomato was thought to be poisonous.

8. Since it was first imported into Australia many years ago, the rabbit has become a serious pest because it has no natural enemies there.

◇ **PRACTICE 2. Modifying phrases. (Charts 18-1 → 18-3)**
Directions: <u>Underline</u> the subject of the adverb clause and the subject of the main clause. Change the adverb clauses to modifying phrases, if possible.

1. While <u>Sam</u> was driving to work in the rain, <u>his car</u> got a flat tire. → *(no change)*

2. While <u>Sam</u> was driving to work, <u>he</u> had a flat tire.
   → *While driving to work, Sam had a flat tire.*

3. Before Nick left on his trip, his son gave him a big hug and a kiss.

4. Before Nick left on his trip, he gave his itinerary to his secretary.

5. After Tom had worked hard in the garden all afternoon, he took a shower and then went to the movies with his friends.

6. After Sunita had made a delicious chicken curry for her friends, they wanted the recipe.

7. Before a friend tries to do something hard, an American may say "Break a leg!" to wish him or her good luck.

8. Emily always straightens her desk before she leaves the office at the end of the day.

◇ **PRACTICE 3. Verb forms in adverb clauses and modifying phrases. (Charts 18-1 → 18-3)**
Directions: Complete the sentences with the correct forms of the verbs in parentheses.

1. a. Before *(leave)* _____leaving_____ on his trip, Tom renewed his passport.

   b. Before Tom *(leave)* _____left_____ on his trip, he renewed his passport.

2. a. After Thomas Edison *(invent)* ___invented/had invented___ the light bulb, he went on to create many other useful inventions.

   b. After *(invent)* ___inventing/having invented___ the light bulb, Thomas Edison went on to create many other useful inventions.

3. a. While *(work)* _____ with uranium ore, Marie Curie discovered two new elements, radium and polonium.

   b. While she *(work)* _____ with uranium ore, Marie Curie discovered two new elements, radium and polonium.

4. a. Before an astronaut *(fly)* _____ on a space mission, s/he will have undergone thousands of hours of training.

   b. Before *(fly)* _____ on a space mission, an astronaut will have undergone thousands of hours of training.

5. a. After they *(study)* _____ the stars, the ancient Mayans in Central America developed a very accurate solar calendar.

   b. After *(study)* _____ the stars, the ancient Mayans in Central America developed a very accurate solar calendar.

6. a. Since *(learn)* _____ that cigarettes cause cancer, many people have stopped smoking.

   b. Since they *(learn)* _____ that cigarettes cause cancer, many people have stopped smoking.

7. a. Aspirin can be poisonous when it *(take)* _____ in excessive amounts.

   b. Aspirin can be poisonous when *(take)* _____ in excessive amounts.

8. a. When *(take)* _____ aspirin, you should be sure to follow the directions on the bottle.

   b. When you *(take)* _____ aspirin, you should be sure to follow the directions on the bottle.

9. a. I took a wrong turn while I *(drive)* _____ to my uncle's house and ended up back where I started.

   b. I took a wrong turn while *(drive)* _____ to my uncle's house and ended up back where I started.

◇ **PRACTICE 4. Modifying phrases. (Charts 18-3 and 18-4)**
   Directions: Combine the two sentences, making a modifying phrase out of the first sentence, if possible.

   1. Larry didn't want to disturb his sleeping wife. He tiptoed out of the room.
      → *Not wanting to disturb his sleeping wife, Larry tiptoed out of the room.*

   2. Larry didn't want to disturb his sleeping wife. She needed to catch up on her sleep.
      → *(no change)*

   3. I misunderstood the directions to the hotel. I arrived one hour late for the dinner party.

   4. I misunderstood the directions to the hotel. The taxi driver didn't know how to get there either.

   5. The taxi driver misunderstood my directions to the hotel. He took me to the wrong place.

   6. Ann remembered that she hadn't turned off the oven. She went directly home.

   7. I met Gina after work. She suggested playing tennis.

   8. My family and I live in the Pacific Northwest, where it rains a great deal. We are accustomed to cool, damp weather.

◇ **PRACTICE 5. Modifying phrases. (Charts 18-1 → 18-5)**
   Directions: Make sentences that combine a modifying phrase with a main clause. Write the capital letter of the most logical main clause to complete the sentence. Use each capital letter only once.

Modifying phrases	**Main clauses**
1. Trying to understand the physics problem, <u>E</u>	A. the desperate woman grasped a floating log after the boat capsized.
2. Since injuring my arm, _____	B. I collapsed in my chair for a rest.
3. Fighting for her life, _____	C. the taxi driver caused a multiple-car accident.
4. Wanting to ask a question, _____	D. carefully proofread all your answers.
5. Exhausted after washing the windows, _____	✔ E. the students repeated the experiment.
6. Not wanting to disturb the manager, _____	F. the athletes waved to the cheering crowd.
7. Upon hearing the announcement that their plane was delayed, _____	G. the little girl raised her hand.
8. Talking with the employees after work, _____	H. the manager learned of their dissatisfaction with their jobs.
9. Attempting to enter the freeway, _____	I. the passengers angrily walked back to the ticket counter.
10. Currently selling at record-low prices, _____	J. I haven't been able to play tennis.
11. Stepping onto the platform to receive their medals, _____	K. gold is considered a good investment.
12. Before turning in your exam paper, _____	L. the worker in charge of Section B of the assembly line told the assistant manager about the problem.

◇ **PRACTICE 6. Modifying phrases with *upon*. (Chart 18-5)**
Directions: Write completions using the ideas in the given list.

> *She learned the problem was not at all serious.*
> *She was told she got it.*
> *He heard these words.*
> *He investigated the cause.*
> ✔ *I arrived at the airport.*
> *I reached the other side of the lake.*

1. It had been a long, uncomfortable trip. Upon ___*arriving at the airport*___, I quickly unfastened my seat belt and stood in the aisle waiting my turn to disembark.

2. I rented a small fishing boat last weekend, but I ended up doing more rowing than fishing. The motor died halfway across the lake, so I had to row to shore. It was a long distance away. Upon _____, I was exhausted.

3. At first, we thought the fire had been caused by lightning. However, upon _____ _____, the fire chief determined it had been caused by faulty electrical wiring.

4. Amy felt terrible. She was sure she had some dread disease, so she went to the doctor for some tests. Upon _____, she was extremely relieved.

5. Janet wanted that scholarship with all her heart and soul. Upon _____ _____, she jumped straight up in the air and let out a scream of happiness.

◇ **PRACTICE 7. Modifying phrases. (Charts 18-1 → 18-5)**
Directions: Write "**I**" if the sentence is INCORRECT. Write "**C**" if the sentence is CORRECT.
Reminder: A modifying phrase must modify the subject of the sentence.

1. __I__ While taking a trip across Europe this summer, Jane's camera suddenly quit working.

2. __C__ When using a microwave oven for the first time, read the instructions carefully about the kind of dish you can use.

3. _____ Having been given their instructions, the teacher told her students to begin working on the test.

4. _____ After receiving the Nobel Peace Prize in 1979, Mother Teresa returned to Calcutta, India, to work and live among the poor, the sick, and the dying.

5. _____ Having studied Greek for several years, Sarah's pronunciation was easy to understand.

6. _____ Since returning to her country after graduation, Maria's parents have enjoyed having all their children home again.

7. _____ While bicycling across the United States, the wheels on my bike had to be replaced several times.

8. _____ When told he would have to have surgery, the doctor reassured Bob that he wouldn't have to miss more than a week of work.

9. _____ Upon hearing the bad news, tears began to flow from her eyes.

10. _____ Before driving across a desert, be sure that your car has good tires as well as enough oil, water, and gas to last the trip.

◇ **PRACTICE 8. TEST A: Connecting ideas. (Chapters 16 → 18)**

Directions: Choose the correct answer.

Example: ___B___ I get angry and upset, I try to take ten deep breaths.
   A. Until   B. Whenever   C. Whereas   D. For

1. _____ Paul brings the money for our lunch, we'll go right down to the cafeteria.
   A. Since   B. As soon as   C. Now that   D. Until

2. The first time I went swimming in deep water, I sank to the bottom like a rock. _____
   I've learned to stay afloat, I feel better about the water, but I still can't swim well.
   A. As soon as   B. The first time   C. When   D. Now that

3. It's obvious that neither the workers _____ to fight the new rules.
   A. nor the manager intend   C. nor the manager intends
   B. intend nor the manager   D. intend nor the manager intends

4. _____ I heard the telephone ring, I didn't answer it.
   A. Because   B. Only if   C. Even though   D. So

5. After _____ to 45 minutes of an extremely boring speech, I found myself nodding off.
   A. was listening   B. listen   C. listening   D. having listen

6. Why did I stay until the end? I am never going to stay and watch a bad movie again!
   _____ I am in that situation, I'm going to leave the theater immediately.
   A. The next time   B. Now that   C. After   D. Until

7. "Why aren't you ready to go?"
   "I am ready."
   "How can that be? It's freezing outside, _____ you're wearing shorts and a T-shirt!"
   A. for   B. so   C. because   D. yet

8. Erin likes to swim, jog, and _____ tennis.
   A. plays   B. play   C. to play   D. playing

9. Since _____ to a warmer and less humid climate, I've had no trouble with my asthma.
   A. upon moving   B. I moving   C. moving   D. I move

10. While _____ to help Tim with his math, I got impatient because he wouldn't pay attention
    to what I was saying.
    A. I am trying   B. having tried   C. I try   D. trying

11. We're going to lose this game _____ our team doesn't start playing better soon.
    A. if   B. unless   C. although   D. whereas

12. Some fish can survive only in salt water, _____ other species can live only in fresh water.
    A. since   B. unless   C. if   D. whereas

13. Joe seemed to be in a good mood, _____ he snapped at me angrily when I asked him to
    join us.
    A. for   B. so   C. yet   D. and

14. _____ Jan arrives, we will have finished this group project.
    A. By the time   B. Until   C. Now that   D. Since

15. For the most part, young children spend their time playing, eating, and _____ a lot.
    A. they sleep   B. sleeping   C. sleep   D. they are sleeping

16. _____ I get back from my next business trip, I'm taking a few days off. I'm worn out!
    A. Every time   B. Since   C. Now that   D. Once

17. _____ unprepared for the exam, I felt sure I would get a low score.
    A. Having   B. Being   C. Because   D. Upon

18. Ever since _____ Ted the bad news, he's been avoiding me.
    A. I told   B. told   C. telling   D. having told

19. _____ my daughter reaches the age of sixteen, she will be able to drive.
    A. Having   B. Since   C. Once   D. Because

20. Matt will enjoy skiing more the next time he goes to the Alps _____ he has had skiing lessons.
    A. unless   B. before   C. now that   D. and

◇ **PRACTICE 9. TEST B: Connecting ideas. (Chapters 16 → 18)**

Directions: Choose the correct answer.

Example: ___B___ I get angry and upset, I try to take ten deep breaths.
   A. Until   B. Whenever   C. whereas   D. For

1. Before _____ a promotion and transfer to another city, I will discuss it at length with my
   whole family to be sure that everyone will be able to adjust to the change.
   A. accept   C. having been accepted
   B. accepted   D. accepting

2. The flowers will soon start to bloom _____ winter is gone and the weather is beginning to
   get warmer.
   A. even if   B. now that   C. so   D. even though

3. Only if you promise to study hard _____ to tutor you.
   A. will I agree   B. agree I   C. I agree   D. I will agree

4. Great white sharks are dangerous to _____ will attack without warning.
   A. humans, they   C. humans. Because they
   B. humans   D. humans. They

5. _____ the need to finish this project soon, I want you to work on this overtime for the
   next few days.
   A. Because   B. Despite   C. Because of   D. Even though

6. _____ the secret of how to make silk remained inside Asia, Europeans were forced to pay
   incredibly high sums of money for this mysterious material to be brought overland to
   Europe.
   A. Although   B. Only if   C. Since   D. Until

7. Jack insisted that he didn't need any help, _____ I helped him anyway.
   A. and   B. so   C. for   D. but

8. _____ by the swimming pool, I realized I was getting sunburned.
   A. Because   C. While I am lying
   B. Lying   D. Even though I was lying

9. _____ it was a formal dinner party, James wore his blue jeans.
   A. Since   C. In the event that
   B. Even though   D. Until

10. Ancient Egyptians mummified their dead through the use of chemicals, _____ ancient
    Peruvians mummified their dead through natural processes by putting dead bodies in
    extremely dry desert caves.
    A. whereas   B. because   C. even though   D. whether or not

11. Mr. Jackson hopes to avoid surgery. He will not agree to the operation _____ he is
    convinced that it is absolutely necessary.
    A. in the event that   C. if
    B. unless   D. only if

12. Some English words have the same pronunciation _____ they are spelled differently, for example, *dear* and *deer.*
    A. unless   B. since   C. even though   D. only if

13. Both my books _____ from my room last night.
    A. were stolen and my wallet   C. and my wallet stolen
    B. and my wallet were stolen   D. and my wallet was stolen

14. When _____ a dictionary, you need to be able to understand the symbols and abbreviations it contains.
    A. having used   B. use   C. to use   D. using

15. You must obey the speed limits on public roads. They are designed to keep you safe. You shouldn't exceed the speed limit _____ you are an experienced race car driver.
    A. even if   B. only if   C. if   D. in the event that

16. My nose got sunburned _____ I wore a hat with a wide brim to shade my face.
    A. if   B. since   C. because   D. even though

17. Do you like jazz? You should go to the jazz festival _____ you like that kind of music.
    A. if   B. unless   C. although   D. while

18. Only if you get to the theater early _____ a chance to get a ticket for tonight's performance.
    A. you will have   B. have   C. will you have   D. you have

19. The bread was old and stale, _____ Martha ate it anyway.
    A. and   B. so   C. for   D. but

20. _____ you're better at numbers than I am, why don't you take over as treasurer of the organization?
    A. Since   B. Only if   C. For that   D. Unless

CHAPTER 19

Connectives That Express Cause and Effect, Contrast, and Condition

◇ **PRACTICE 1.** *Because* vs. *because of.* (Charts 17-2 and 19-1)
   Directions: Complete the sentences with either *because* or *because of.*

   1. We delayed our trip __because of__ the bad weather.

   2. Sue's eyes were red __because__ she had been crying.

   3. The water in most rivers is unsafe to drink _____ pollution.

   4. The water in most rivers is unsafe to drink _____ it is polluted.

   5. Some people think Harry succeeded in business _____ his charming
      personality rather than his business skills.

   6. You can't enter this secured area _____ you don't have an official permit.

   7. My lecture notes were incomplete _____ the instructor talked too fast.

   8. It's unsafe to travel in that country _____ the ongoing civil war.

◇ **PRACTICE 2.** *Because* vs. *therefore.* (Charts 17-2, 19-1, and 19-2)
   Directions: Complete the sentences with either *because* or *therefore.*

   1. Matt didn't go to work yesterday __because__ he didn't feel well.

   2. Matt didn't feel well. __Therefore__, he didn't go to work yesterday.

   3. Sharon hid her feelings from everyone. _____, no one suspected the deep
      emotional pain she was suffering.

   4. No one ever knows what's going on inside of Sharon _____ she hides her
      feelings behind a mask of smiles.

   5. _____ young Joseph was an inquisitive student, he was always liked by his
      teachers.

   6. The television broadcast was interrupted in the middle of the eighth inning;
      _____, most of the audience missed the conclusion of the baseball game.

◇ **PRACTICE 3. Showing cause and effect. (Charts 17-2, 19-1, and 19-2)**

PART I. Complete the sentences with *because of, because,* or *therefore*. Add any necessary punctuation and capitalization.

1. ___Because___ it rained, we stayed home.

2. It rained __. Therefore,__ we stayed home.

3. We stayed home ___because of___ the bad weather.

4. The hurricane was moving directly toward a small coastal town _____

   all residents were advised to move inland until it passed.

5. The residents moved inland _____ the hurricane.

6. _____ the hurricane was moving directly toward the town all residents

   were advised to move inland.

7. Piranhas, which are found in the Amazon River, are ferocious and bloodthirsty fish. When

   they attack in great numbers, they can devour an entire cow in several minutes

   _____ their extremely sharp teeth.

PART II. Complete the sentence with *due to, since,* or *consequently*. Add any necessary punctuation and capitalization.

8. _____ his poor eyesight John has to sit in the front row in class.

9. _____ John has poor eyesight he has to sit in the front row.

10. John has poor eyesight _____ he has to sit in the front row.

11. Sarah is afraid of heights _____ she will not walk across a bridge.

12. Sarah will not walk across a bridge _____ her fear of heights.

13. Mark is overweight _____ his doctor has advised him to exercise

    regularly.

14. _____ a diamond is extremely hard it can be used to cut glass.

◇ **PRACTICE 4. Periods and commas. (Charts 16-3 and 19-3)**

Directions: Punctuate the sentences properly, using periods and commas. Capitalize as appropriate.

1. Edward missed the final exam. **T**therefore, he failed the course.*

2. Edward failed the course because he missed the final exam. *(no change)*

3. Edward missed the final exam. **H**he simply forgot to go to it.**

---

*The use of a semicolon is also possible:
  Edward missed the final exam; therefore, he failed the course.

**The use of a semicolon is also possible:
  Edward missed the final exam; he simply forgot to go to it.

4. Because we forgot to make a reservation we couldn't get a table at our favorite restaurant last night.

5. The waitress kept dropping trays full of dishes therefore she was fired.

6. The waiter kept forgetting customers' orders so he was fired.

7. Ron is an unpleasant dinner companion because of his uncouth table manners.

8. The needle has been around since prehistoric times the button was invented about 2000 years ago the zipper wasn't invented until 1890.

9. It is possible for wildlife observers to identify individual zebras because the patterns of stripes on each zebra are unique no two zebras are alike.

10. When students are learning to type, they often practice the sentence "The quick brown fox jumps over the lazy dog" because it contains all the letters of the alphabet.

◇ **PRACTICE 5. Such . . . that and so . . . that. (Chart 19-4)**
   Directions: Add **such** or **so** to the following sentences.

1. It was ___such___ a hot day that we canceled our tennis game.

2. The test was ___so___ easy that everyone got a high score.

3. The movie was _____ bad that we left early.

4. It was _____ a bad movie that we left early.

5. Professor James is _____ a stern taskmaster that lazy students won't take his class.

6. The restaurant patron at the table near us was _____ belligerent that we all felt embarrassed, especially when he swept everything off the table and demanded his money back.

7. The intricate metal lacework on the Eiffel Tower in Paris was _____ complicated that the structure took more than two and a half years to complete.

8. Charles and his brother are _____ hard-working carpenters that I'm sure they'll make a success of their new business.

9. The children had _____ much fun at the carnival that they begged to go again.

10. I feel like I have _____ little energy that I wonder if I'm getting sick.

◇ **PRACTICE 6. Such . . . that and so . . . that. (Chart 19-4)**
   Directions: Combine the sentences by using **so . . . that** or **such . . . that**.

1. We took a walk. It was a nice day.
   → *It was such a nice day that we took a walk.*

2. The weather was hot. You could fry an egg on the sidewalk.

3. I couldn't understand her. She talked too fast.

4. It was an expensive car. We couldn't afford to buy it.

5. I don't feel like going to class. We're having beautiful weather.

6. Grandpa held me tightly when he hugged me. I couldn't breathe for a moment.

7. There were few people at the meeting. It was canceled.

8. The classroom has comfortable chairs. The students find it easy to fall asleep.

9. Ted couldn't get to sleep last night. He was worried about the exam.

10. Jerry got angry. He put his fist through the wall.

11. I have many problems. I can use all the help you can give me.

12. The tornado struck with great force. It lifted automobiles off the ground.

13. I can't figure out what this sentence says. His handwriting is illegible.

14. David has too many girlfriends. He can't remember all of their names.

15. Too many people came to the meeting. There were not enough seats for everyone.

◇ **PRACTICE 7. *So that.* (Chart 19-5)**
Directions: Combine the ideas using *so that*.

1. Rachel wanted to watch the news. She turned on the TV.
   → *Rachel turned on the TV so that she could watch the news.*

2. Alex wrote down the time and date of his appointment. He didn't want to forget to go.
   → *Alex wrote down the time and date of his appointment so that he wouldn't forget to go.*

3. Nancy is carrying extra courses every semester. She wants to graduate early.

4. Jason wants to travel in Europe. He's tired of work and school and is planning to take a semester off.

5. Suzanne didn't want to disturb her roommate. She lowered the volume on the TV set.

6. Whenever we are planning a vacation, we call a travel agent. We are able to get expert advice on our itinerary.

7. It's a good idea for you to learn how to type. You'll be able to type your own papers when you go to the university.

8. Lynn wanted to make sure that she didn't forget to take her book back to the library. She tied a string around her finger.

9. Ed took some change from his pocket. He wanted to buy a newspaper.

10. I wanted to listen to the news while I was making dinner. I turned on the TV.

11. I unplugged the phone. I didn't want to be interrupted while I was working.

12. Yesterday Linda was driving on the highway when her car started making strange noises. After she pulled over to the side of the road, she raised the hood of her car in order to make sure that other drivers knew that she had car trouble.

◇ **PRACTICE 8. Cause and effect. (Charts 16-3, 17-2, and 19-1 → 19-5)**

Directions: Choose the correct completion.

Example: ___B___ I was tired, I went to bed.
    A. Because of   B. Since   C. For   D. Due to

1. The workers have gone on strike. _____, all production has ceased.
    A. Because   B. So that   C. Now that   D. Therefore

2. A small fish needs camouflage to hide itself _____ its enemies cannot find it.
    A. so that   B. because   C. therefore   D. due to

3. Our apartment building has had two robberies in the last month, _____ I'm going to put an extra lock on the door and install a telephone in my bedroom.
    A. now that   B. so that   C. so   D. since

4. The Chippewas are Native North Americans. Their language is one of the most complex in the world, _____ it contains more than 6,000 verb forms.
    A. consequently   B. so   C. so that   D. for

5. _____ the bad grease stain on the carpet, we had to rearrange the furniture before the company arrived.
    A. Because   B. Now that   C. For   D. Because of

6. The price of airline tickets has gone down recently. _____ the tickets cost less, more people are flying than before.
    A. Consequently   B. Because of   C. Because   D. For

7. Let's ask our teacher how to solve this problem _____ we can't agree on the answer.
    A. since   B. because of   C. consequently   D. so

8. The fire raged out of control. It got _____ bad that more firefighters had to be called in.
    A. such   B. therefore   C. so   D. so that

9. Dolphins are sometimes caught and killed in commercial fishing nets _____ they often swim in schools with other fish, such as tuna.
    A. due to   B. because   C. so   D. therefore

10. We can finally afford to trade in the old car for a new one _____ I've gotten the raise I've been waiting for.
    A. so that   B. consequently   C. now that   D. so

11. Two of the factories in our small town have closed. _____, unemployment is high.
    A. Consequently   B. Because   C. So that   D. For

12. _____ I had nothing for lunch but an apple, I ate dinner early.
    A. For   B. Since   C. Due to   D. Therefore

13. I needed to finish the marathon race _____ I could prove that I had the strength and stamina to do it. I didn't care whether I won or not.
    A. because of   B. so that   C. for   D. therefore

14. The Eskimo* way of life changed dramatically during the 1800s _____ the introduction of firearms and the influx of large numbers of European whalers and fur traders.
    A. because   B. for   C. due to   D. so

15. During extremely hot weather, elephants require both mud and water to keep their skin cool _____ they have no sweat glands.
    A. and   B. because of   C. so   D. due to the fact that

◇ **PRACTICE 9. Showing contrast: punctuation. (Chart 19-6)**
   Directions: Add commas, periods, and capital letters as necessary. Do not add or omit any words. Do not change the order of the words.

   1. Annie told the truth**,** but no one believed her.

   2. Annie told the truth**.** **H** ~~h~~owever, no one believed her.**

   3. Even though Annie told the truth no one believed her.

   4. No one believed Annie even though she told the truth.

   5. Annie told the truth yet no one believed her.

   6. Annie told the truth nevertheless no one believed her.

   7. In spite of the fact that Annie told the truth no one believed her.

   8. No one believed Annie despite the fact that she told the truth.

   9. Even though all of my family friends have advised me not to travel abroad during this time of political turmoil I'm leaving next week to begin a trip around the world.

   10. Some people think great strides have been made in cleaning up the environment in much of the world however others think the situation is much worse than it was twenty years ago.

◇ **PRACTICE 10. *Despite/in spite of* vs. *even though/although*. (Chart 19-6)**
   Directions: Choose the correct completions.

   1. a. *Even though, Despite* her doctor warned her, Carol has continued to smoke nearly three packs of cigarettes a day.

      b. *Even though, Despite* her doctor's warnings, Carol has continued to smoke nearly three packs of cigarettes a day.

      c. *Even though, Despite* the warnings her doctor gave her, Carol continues to smoke.

      d. *Even though, Despite* the fact that her doctor warned her of dangers to her health, Carol continues to smoke.

      e. *Even though, Despite* she has been warned about the dangers of smoking by her doctor, Carol continues to smoke.

   _____
   *Eskimos are people who live in the Arctic regions of northern Alaska, northern Canada, and Greenland.
   **Also possible: *Annie told the truth; however, no one believed her.*

2. a. *Although, In spite of* an approaching storm, the two climbers continued their trek up the mountain.

   b. *Although, In spite of* a storm was approaching, the two climbers continued their trek.

   c. *Although, In spite of* there was an approaching storm, the two climbers continued up the mountain.

   d. *Although, In spite of* the storm that was approaching the mountain area, the two climbers continued their trek.

   e. *Although, In spite of* the fact that a storm was approaching the mountain area, the two climbers continued their trek.

3. a. *Although, Despite* his many hours of practice, George failed his driving test for the third time.

   b. *Although, Despite* he had practiced for many hours, George failed his driving test for the third time.

   c. *Although, Despite* practicing for many hours, George failed his driving test again.

   d. *Although, Despite* his mother and father spent hours with him in the car trying to teach him how to drive, George failed his driving test repeatedly.

   e. *Although, Despite* his mother and father's efforts to teach him how to drive, George failed his driving test.

4. a. *Even though, In spite of* repeated crop failures due to drought, the villagers are refusing to leave their traditional homeland for resettlement in other areas.

   b. *Even though, In spite of* their crops have failed repeatedly due to drought, the villagers are refusing to leave their traditional homeland for resettlement in other areas.

c. The villagers refuse to leave *even though, in spite of* the drought.

d. The villagers refuse to leave *even though, in spite of* the drought seriously threatens their food supply.

e. The villagers refuse to leave *even though, in spite of* the threat to their food supply because of the continued drought.

f. The villagers refuse to leave *even though, in spite of* the threat to their food supply is serious because of the continued drought.

g. The villagers refuse to leave *even though, in spite of* their food supply is threatened.

h. The villagers refuse to leave *even though, in spite of* their threatened food supply.

◇ **PRACTICE 11. Using *in spite of/despite* and *even though/though/although.* (Chart 19-6)**
    Directions: Choose the phrase from the list that best completes each sentence. Use each completion only once.

```
    A. its many benefits
  ✔B. its inherent dangers
    C. it has been shown to be safe
    D. it has been shown to cause birth defects and sometimes death
    E. his fear of heights
    F. he is afraid of heights
    G. he is normally quite shy and sometimes inarticulate
    H. an inability to communicate well in any language besides English
    I. having excellent skills in the job category they were trying to fill
    J. he had the necessary qualifications
```

1. In spite of ___B___, nuclear energy is a clean and potentially inexhaustible source of energy.

2. In spite of _____, Carl enjoyed his helicopter trip over the Grand Canyon in Arizona.

3. Because of his age, John was not hired even though _____.

4. Although _____, Mark rode an elevator to the top of the World Trade Center in New York for the magnificent view.

5. Although _____, many people avoid using a microwave oven for fear of its rays.

6. Jack usually has little trouble making new friends in another country despite _____.

7. In spite of _____, the use of chemotherapy to treat cancer has many severe side effects.

8. Though _____, Bob managed to give an excellent presentation at the board meeting.

9. Jerry continued to be denied a promotion despite _____.

10. DDT is still used in many countries as a primary insecticide even though _____.

◇ **PRACTICE 12. Direct contrast. (Chart 19-7)**
Directions: Connect the given ideas, using the words in parentheses. Add commas, periods, semicolons, and capital letters as necessary.

1. *(while)* red is bright and lively gray is a dull color
   → *Red is bright and lively, while gray is a dull color.* OR
   → *While red is bright and lively, gray is a dull color.*

2. *(on the other hand)* Jane is insecure and unsure of herself her sister is full of self-confidence

3. *(while)* a rock is heavy a feather is light

4. *(whereas)* some children are unruly others are quiet and obedient

5. *(on the other hand)* language and literature classes are easy and enjoyable for Alex math and science courses are difficult for him

6. *(however)* strikes can bring improvements in wages and working conditions strikes can also cause loss of jobs and bankruptcy

◇ **PRACTICE 13. Cause and effect; showing contrast. (Charts 16-3, 17-2, and 19-1 → 19-7)**
Directions: Show the relationship between the ideas by adding any of the following expressions, as appropriate. There may be more than one possible completion.

because	because of	while/whereas	on the other hand
since	due to	nevertheless	in spite of
now that	even though	however	despite
therefore	although		

1. It was still hot in the room ___even though/although___ I had turned on the air conditioner.

2. Several people in the crowd became ill and fainted ___due to/because of___ the extreme heat.

3. The gardener trimmed the branches on the cherry tree _____ I asked him not to.

4. The meat of the puffer fish can cause paralysis or even death if it is improperly prepared. _____, it remains a delicacy in Japan for brave diners.

5. _____ everyone disagreed with him, Brian went ahead with his original plan for the company.

6. The first mention of the game of chess appears in an Indian text written almost 1500 years ago. _____ its ancient beginnings, it remains one of the most widely played games in the world today.

7. Alice heard a siren and saw the flashing lights of a police car in her rear-view mirror. _____, she quickly pulled over to the side of the road and stopped.

8. Most adults carry around certain attitudes and prejudices about the world around them. Most children, _____, enter new situations without such preconceived notions.

9. They often have to close all of the ski areas in the mountains _____ severe weather conditions and avalanche danger.

10. _____ paper was first developed by the ancient Chinese, its English name comes from the word *papyrus,* the name of an Egyptian water plant.

11. The supervisor must know what everyone in the department is doing _____ all responsibility for error will fall on her shoulders.

12. _____ aspirin is relatively safe for most adults, it should be administered very carefully to children, if at all. It can be dangerous to children's health.

13. The peanut is used today to make everything from cosmetics to explosives _____ the pioneering scientific work of George Washington Carver in the 1910s and 1920s.

14. In ancient China, yellow was considered to be an imperial color. _____, only the emperor was allowed to wear it. No one else could have yellow clothing of any kind.

15. _____ the abacus had been in use in Asia since ancient times, many in the Western world credited 19-year-old Blaise Pascal, a Frenchman, with inventing the first calculating machine in 1642.

16. _____ she thought she heard the telephone ringing, Marge turned the TV down—only to discover it had been a telephone on the show she was watching.

◇ **PRACTICE 14. Using *otherwise*. (Chart 19-8)**
   Directions: Make two sentences. Show the relationship between them by using *otherwise.* In the first sentence, use a modal auxiliary or phrasal modal: *should, had better, have to, must, etc.*

   1. If you don't eat less and get more exercise, you won't lose weight.
      → *You should (had better/have to/must) eat less and get more exercise. Otherwise, you won't lose weight.*

   2. The children can watch TV tonight only if they finish all of their chores.
      → *The children have to (had better/should/must) finish all of their chores. Otherwise, they cannot watch TV tonight.*

   3. Unless you speak up now, the boss will go ahead without knowing that you don't agree.

   4. If you don't stop at the store on your way home from work, we won't have anything to eat for dinner tonight.

   5. Unless you think it through very carefully, you won't come up with the right answer.

   6. If we don't catch any fish this morning, we're going to have beans for dinner again.

7. It's going to be very difficult to finish on time if you don't get someone to help you.

8. Maria is probably going to lose her job unless she finds a way to convince the boss that the error was unavoidable.

◇ **PRACTICE 15. Expressing conditions. (Charts 17-6 → 17-9 and 19-8)**
   Directions: Complete the sentences with any appropriate form of the verb **pass**.

   1. Keith will graduate if he ___*passes*___ all of his courses.

   2. Sam won't graduate if he ___*doesn't pass*___ all of his courses.

   3. Ed won't graduate unless he _____ all of his courses.

   4. Sue will graduate only if she _____ all of her courses.

   5. Jessica will graduate even if she _____ all of her courses.

   6. Alex won't graduate even if he _____ all of his courses.

   7. Jennifer will graduate unless she _____ all of her courses.

   8. Amy won't graduate in the event that she _____ all of her courses.

   9. Jerry _____ all of his courses. Otherwise, he won't graduate.

   10. Carolyn _____ all of her courses, or else she won't graduate.

Directions: Choose the best completion.

1. I have to eat breakfast in the morning. _____, I get grouchy and hungry before my lunch break.
   A. Consequently   B. And   C. Otherwise   D. However

2. My mouth is burning! This is _____ spicy food that I don't think I can finish it.
   A. such   B. so   C. very   D. too

3. I couldn't use the pay phone, _____ I didn't have any coins with me.
   A. yet   B. despite   C. for   D. even though

4. Bats are fascinating _____ have many interesting and amazing qualities.
   A. animals. Therefore, they   C. animals. They
   B. animals, they   D. animals. Because they

5. I need to find an apartment before I can move. _____ I can find one in the next week or so, I will move to Chicago the first of next month.
   A. If   B. Even if   C. Whether   D. Only if

6. Sam and I would love to meet you at a restaurant tonight, but we can do that _____ we can find a babysitter.
   A. if   B. unless   C. only if   D. even if

7. _____ want to take a train trip across western Canada, but my traveling companion wants to fly to Mexico City for our vacation.
   A. Although I   B. Even if I   C. I   D. Despite I

8. Timmy doesn't do well in school _____ his inability to concentrate on any one thing for longer than a minute or two.
   A. as   B. because of   C. because   D. therefore

9. Tony spent _____ money buying movie tickets that he didn't have enough left to buy a soft drink or candy bar.
   A. such   B. a lot of   C. too much   D. so much

10. You should learn how to change a tire on your car _____ you can handle an emergency situation if necessary.
    A. so that   B. if   C. for that   D. therefore

11. Cars have become much more complicated. _____, mechanics need more training than in the past.
    A. Because   B. Therefore   C. So that   D. For

12. Not wanting to be late my first day of class, _____ to school after I missed my bus.
    A. so I ran   B. because I ran   C. I ran   D. therefore, I ran

13. It was raining _____ I couldn't go outside.
    A. because   B. so hard that   C. so that   D. too hard that

14. The Northern Hemisphere has mostly westerly winds _____ the rotation of the earth toward the east.
    A. due to   B. because   C. therefore   D. so

15. Emily is motivated to study _____ she knows that a good education can improve her life.
    A. therefore   B. because of   C. because   D. so

16. Sonia broke her leg in two places. _____, she had to wear a cast and use crutches for three months.
    A. Nevertheless   B. Consequently   C. For that   D. Because

17. Carol showed up for the meeting _____ I asked her not to be there.
    A. even though   B. despite   C. because of   D. because

18. Peter works hard at everything he does. His brother, _____, seldom puts out much effort.
    A. on the other hand   C. even though
    B. otherwise   D. consequently

19. The road will remain safe _____ the flood washes out the bridge.
    A. as long as   B. unless   C. if   D. since

20. _____ I can't make the presentation myself, I've asked my assistant to be prepared to do it for me.
    A. For   C. Only if
    B. In the event that   D. On the other hand

21. I have to go to the meeting _____ I want to or not.
    A. because   B. whether   C. even though   D. only if

22. I asked Angela to run the office while I'm gone _____ I know I can depend on her.
    A. unless   B. since   C. Although   D. so that

23. I think I did okay in my speech last night _____ I'd had almost no sleep for 24 hours.
    A. in spite of   B. unless   C. so that   D. despite the fact that

24. I talked to Anna throughout the evening, _____ nothing I said changed her opinion.
    A. yet   B. and   C. otherwise   D. so that

25. After getting home from elementary school, _____.
    A. our house buzzes with the children's many activities
    B. the dog greets the children at the front door with wagging tail
    C. the children have an hour to play before they begin their homework
    D. the school bus drops the children at the corner near their house

Directions: Choose the best completion.

1. _____ the extremely bad weather in the mountains, my friends decided not to cancel their trip across the mountain pass.
   A. Because of   B. In spite of   C. Even if   D. Even though

2. Even though a duck lives on water, it stays dry _____ the oil on its feathers, which prevents water from reaching its skin.
   A. because of   B. since   C. because   D. for

3. Alex cannot express himself clearly and correctly in writing. He will never advance in his job _____ he improves his language skills.
   A. otherwise   B. if   C. only if   D. unless

4. _____ there was no electricity, I was able to read because I had a candle.
   A. Unless   B. Even though   C. Even   D. Only if

5. A fire must have a readily available supply of oxygen. _____, it will stop burning.
   A. Consequently   B. Therefore   C. Otherwise   D. However

6. I studied Spanish for four years in high school. _____, I had trouble talking with people when I was traveling in Spain.
   A. Therefore   C. Otherwise
   B. On the other hand   D. Nonetheless

7. I'm sorry you've decided not to go with us on the river trip, but _____ you change your mind, there will still be enough room on the boat for you.
   A. even   C. in the event that
   B. nevertheless   D. although

8. I like to keep the windows open at night no matter how cold it gets. My wife, _____, prefers a warm bedroom with all windows tightly shut.
   A. nevertheless   C. on the other hand
   B. consequently   D. whereas

9. You must lend me the money for the trip. _____, I won't be able to go.
   A. Consequently   B. Nevertheless   C. Otherwise   D. Although

10. I don't understand why, but my neighbor Mr. Morrow doesn't seem to like me. He never smiles at me or speaks to me _____ the many efforts I have made to be friendly and neighborly.
    A. because of   B. in spite of   C. for   D. so

11. _____ the salary meets my expectations, I will accept the job offer.
    A. Due to   B. Even if   C. If   D. Unless

12. Camels have either one hump or two humps. The Arabian camel has one hump. The Bactrian camel, _____, has two humps.
    A. nevertheless   B. however   C. therefore   D. otherwise

13. Ms. Moore, the school counselor, has had years of experience dealing with student problems. _____, she is sometimes confronted by a problem that she cannot handle by herself.

    A. Therefore   B. Nevertheless   C. Otherwise   D. On the other hand

14. Right now all the seats on that flight are taken, sir. _____ there is a cancelation, I will call you.

    A. In the event that   C. Unless
    B. Nevertheless   D. Even if

15. A newborn baby can neither walk nor crawl. A newborn antelope, _____, can run within minutes of birth.

    A. however   B. nevertheless   C. otherwise   D. even though

16. Jason has become _____ famous that he now ignores his old friends. He shouldn't do that.

    A. such   B. so   C. so much   D. too

17. Joan worked in a vineyard last summer _____ money for school expenses.

    A. because to earn   C. for she earned
    B. so she earns   D. so that she could earn

18. Watching the children fly their kites in the park, _____.

    A. suddenly a gust of wind blew my hat off my head
    B. one of the kites got stuck in a tree
    C. I thought of the times long ago when I did the same thing
    D. it looked like a lot of fun

19. I guess I'm a soft touch. I just lent Jan some money for lunch _____ she never paid me back my last loan.

    A. even though   B. unless   C. or else   D. only if

20. Hundreds of species of Hawaiian flowers have become extinct or rare _____ extensive land development and the grazing of wild goats.

    A. now that   B. due to   C. because   D. for

21. It looks like they're going to succeed _____ their present difficulties.

    A. despite   B. because of   C. even though   D. yet

22. The professor told me that I was doing well, _____ my final grade was awful.

    A. so   B. therefore   C. in spite of   D. yet

23. _____ Beth has a new car, she no longer takes the commuter train to work. She drives to work every day.

    A. Now that   B. While   C. Although   D. In case

24. Our village had _____ money available for education that the schools had to close.

    A. so little   B. such little   C. so much   D. such much

25. I hadn't understood his _____ asked him to repeat what he'd said.

    A. directions. I   C. directions, I
    B. directions because I   D. directions. However, I

CHAPTER 20

Conditional Sentences and Wishes

◇ **PRACTICE 1. Conditional sentences: present/future. (Charts 20-1 → 20-3)**

Directions: Complete the sentences with the correct form of the verbs in parentheses. Some of the sentences are contrary to fact, and some are not.

1. I am not an astronaut. If I *(be)* ___were___ were an astronaut, I *(take)* ___would take___ my camera with me on the rocket ship next month.

2. That sounds like a good job offer. I *(accept)* _____ it if I *(be)* _____ you.

3. Don't throw aerosol cans into a fire. An aerosol can *(explode)* _____ if you *(throw)* _____ it into a fire.

4. It is expensive to call across the ocean. However, if transoceanic telephone calls *(be)* _____ cheap, I *(call)* _____ my family every day and *(talk)* _____ for hours.

5. The teacher was absent today, so class was canceled. If she *(be)* _____ absent again tomorrow, class *(cancel)* _____ tomorrow, too.

6. Sea water is salty. If the oceans *(consist)* _____ of fresh water, there *(be)* _____ plenty of water to irrigate all of the deserts in the world to provide an abundant food supply for the entire population of the earth.

◇ **PRACTICE 2. Conditional sentences: past time. (Chart 20-4)**

Directions: Complete the sentences with the words in parentheses. All of the sentences to complete are contrary to fact.

1. I'm sorry you had to take a cab to the airport. I didn't know you needed a ride. If you *(tell)* ___had told___ me, I *(give)* ___would have given___ you a ride gladly.

2. I got wet because I didn't take my umbrella. However, I *(get, not)* _____ _____ wet if I *(remember)* _____ to take my umbrella with me yesterday.

3. Many people were not satisfied with the leader after he took office. If they *(know)* _____ more about his planned economic program, they *(vote, not)* _____ for him.

4. You made a lot of unnecessary mistakes in your composition. You *(get)* _____ _____ a better grade if you *(use)* _____ either a dictionary or the spell checker on your computer to check your spelling.

5. A: Oh, no! I've lost it!

   B: Lost what?

   A: The address for my job interview this afternoon. I wrote it on a match book.

   B: A match book! If you *(write)* _____ the address in your appointment book where it belongs, you *(lose, not)* _____ it. When are you going to get organized?

6. A: Ann, *(you, take)* _____ that job if you *(know)* _____ _____ that you had to work nights?

   B: No way. I had no idea I'd have to work the late night hours they've had me working.

◇ **PRACTICE 3. Conditional sentences: present/future and past time. (Charts 20-1 → 20-4)**
Directions: Complete the sentences with the words in parentheses.

1. If I *(have)* _____ wings, I *(have to, not)* _____ take an airplane to fly home.

2. *(people, be)* _____ able to fly if they *(have)* _____ feathers instead of hair?

3. This box has got to be in Chicago tomorrow. I'm going to send it by express mail. I'm sure if I *(send)* _____ it today by overnight express, it *(arrive)* _____ _____ in time.

4. I didn't know the Newtons were going to bring two other people to dinner last night. If anyone else *(bring)* _____ an extra guest, we *(have, not)* _____ _____ enough seats at the table.

5. A: I don't understand anything in this class. It's boring. And I'm getting a failing grade.

   B: If I *(feel)* _____ the way you do about it, I *(drop)* _____ _____ the class as soon as possible.

6. I've never understood why people build houses on flood plains. If we *(have)* _____ heavy rains in the spring, the river through my hometown *(rise, always)* _____ _____ above its banks and *(flood)* _____ the low-lying areas of the town. Some houses have been flooded a half-dozen times in the last 20 years.

7. A: I'm exhausted, and we're no closer to a solution to this problem after nine hours of work.

   B: Why don't you go home and get some sleep, and I'll keep working. If I *(discover)* _____ a solution before morning, I *(call)* _____ you immediately. I promise.

8. A: I can't believe that you haven't finished that report. What will I use in the committee meeting at noon today?

   B: I'm really sorry. If I *(know)* _____ you needed it today, I *(stay)* _____ up all night last night and *(finish)* _____ it.

◇ **PRACTICE 4. Conditional sentences. (Charts 20-1 → 20-4)**

Directions: Using the given information, create conditional sentences. Use *if*.

1. I was sick yesterday, so I didn't go to class.
   → *If I hadn't been sick yesterday, I would have gone to class.*

2. Because Alan never eats breakfast, he always overeats at lunch.
   → *If Alan ate breakfast, he wouldn't overeat at lunch.*

3. Kostas was late to his own wedding because his watch was slow.

4. I don't ride the bus to work every morning because it's always so crowded.

5. Sara didn't know that highway 57 was closed, so she didn't take an alternative route.

6. Camille couldn't finish unloading the truck because no one was there to help her.

◇ **PRACTICE 5. Using progressive forms and "mixed time" in conditional sentences. (Charts 20-5 and 20-6)**

Directions: Using the given information, complete the conditional sentences.

1. *It is raining, so we won't finish the game.*
   → If it ___weren't raining___, we ___would finish___ the game.

2. *I didn't eat lunch, and now I'm hungry.*
   → If I ___had eaten___ lunch, I ___wouldn't be___ hungry now.

3. *Bob left his wallet at home this morning, and now he doesn't have any money for lunch.*
   → If Bob _____ his wallet at home this morning, he _____ some money for lunch now.

4. *Carol didn't answer the phone because she was studying.*
   → Carol _____ the phone if she _____.

5. *The sun was shining, so we went to the beach yesterday.*
   → If the sun _____, we _____ to the beach yesterday.

6. *Every muscle in my body aches today because I played basketball for three hours last night.*

→ Every muscle in my body _____ today if I _____

_____ basketball for three hours last night.

7. *Barry stops to shake everyone's hand because he's running for political office.*

→ Barry _____ to shake everyone's hand if he _____

_____ for political office.

8. *We didn't eat all of the turkey at dinner last night, so we have to have turkey again tonight.*

→ If we _____ all of the turkey at dinner last night, we

_____ turkey again tonight.

9. *The music was playing loudly at the restaurant, so I didn't hear everything Mr. Lee said during dinner.*

→ If the music _____ so loudly, I _____

everything Mr. Lee said during dinner.

10. *The library is closing now, so Abdul will have to leave before finishing his research.*

→ If the library _____ now, Abdul _____

_____ before finishing his research.

◇ **PRACTICE 6. Using progressive forms and "mixed time" in conditional sentences. (Charts 20-5 and 20-6)**

Directions: Using the given information, make conditional sentences. Use *if*.

1. The wind is blowing hard, so I won't take the boat out for a ride.
   → *If the wind weren't blowing hard, I would take the boat out for a ride.*

2. I feel better now because you talked to me about my problems last night.

   → *I wouldn't feel better now if you hadn't talked to me about my problems last night.*

3. Ann carried heavy furniture when she helped her friend move. Her back hurts now.

4. Paulo is working on two jobs right now, so he doesn't have time to help you with your remodeling.

5. I wasn't working at the restaurant last night. I didn't wait on your table.

6. Because Diane asked questions every time she didn't understand a problem, she has a good understanding of geometry now.

7. A fallen tree was blocking the road, so we didn't arrive on time.

8. Rita is exhausted today because she didn't get any sleep last night.

9. Olga and Ivan weren't paying attention, so they didn't see the sign marking their exit from the highway.

10. The doctor doesn't really care about his patients. He didn't explain the medical procedure to me before surgery.

◇ **PRACTICE 7. Omitting if. (Chart 20-7)**

Directions: Make sentences with the same meaning by omitting **if**.

1. *If you should need my help, please call.*

   → ____Should you need____ my help, please call.

2. *If I were you, I wouldn't go there.*

   → _____ you, I wouldn't go there.

3. *If I had been offered a job at the law office, I would have gladly accepted.*

   → _____ a job at the law office, I would have gladly accepted.

4. *If anyone should call, would you please take a message?*

   → _____ , would you please take a message?

5. *If I were your doctor, I'd insist that you stop smoking.*

   → _____ your doctor, I'd insist you stop smoking.

6. *They wouldn't have visited her house if they had known about her illness.*

   → They wouldn't have visited her house _____ about her illness.

7. *I would start giving my sister driving lessons if she were just a little older.*

   → I would start giving my sister driving lessons _____ just a little older.

8. *If I had not opened the door when I did, I wouldn't have seen you walk by.*

   → _____ the door when I did, I wouldn't have seen you walk by.

◇ **PRACTICE 8. Omitting if. (Chart 20-7)**

Directions: Make sentences with the same meaning by omitting **if**.

1. If I were your age, I'd do things differently.
   → *Were I your age, I'd do things differently.*

2. If Bob should show up while I'm away, please give him my message.

3. If my uncle had stood up to sing, I'd have been embarrassed.

4. If she were ever in trouble, I'd do anything I could to help her.

5. If the manager should question these figures, have her talk to the bookkeeper.

6. I wouldn't have known about your new job if I hadn't talked to your mother.

◇ **PRACTICE 9. Implied conditions. (Chart 20-8)**

Directions: Notice the conditional verbs in the sentences. Then, using the given information, complete the implied *if*-clauses.

1. *Sara's dad **would have picked** her up, but I forgot to tell him that she needed a ride.*

   → Sara's dad would have picked her up if ____I hadn't forgotten to tell him that____
   ____she needed a ride.____

2. *I **couldn't have made it** without your help.*

   → I couldn't have made it if _____

3. *I opened the door slowly. Otherwise, I **could have hit** someone.*

   → If _____, I could have hit someone.

4. *Doug **would have gone** with me, but he couldn't get time off from work.*

   → Doug would have gone with me if _____

5. *Carol: Why didn't Oscar tell his boss about the problem?*

   *Alice: He **would have gotten** into a lot of trouble.*

   → Oscar would have gotten into a lot of trouble if _____

   _____

◇ **PRACTICE 10. Review: conditional sentences. (Charts 20-1 → 20-8)**
   Directions: Choose the correct completion.

   1. If I could speak Spanish, I _____ next year studying in Mexico.
      A. will spend   C. had spent
      B. would have spent   D. would spend

   2. It would have been a much more serious accident _____ fast at the time.
      A. was she driving   C. she had driven
      B. had she been driving   D. if she drove

   3. "Can I borrow your car for this evening?"
      "Sure, but Nora's using it right now. If she _____ it back in time, you're welcome to borrow it."
      A. brought   B. would bring   C. will bring   D. brings

   4. I didn't get home until well after midnight last night. Otherwise, I _____ your call.
      A. returned   B. had returned   C. would return   D. would have returned

   5. If energy _____ inexpensive and unlimited, many things in the world would be different.
      A. is   B. will be   C. were   D. would be

   6. We _____ the game if we'd had a few more minutes.
      A. could have won   C. had won
      B. won   D. will win

   7. I _____ William with me if I had known you and he didn't get along with each other.
      A. hadn't brought   C. wouldn't have brought
      B. didn't bring   D. won't bring

   8. The lecturer last night didn't know what he was talking about, but if Dr. Mason _____,
      I would have listened carefully.
      A. lectured   C. was lecturing
      B. had been lecturing   D. would lecture

   9. If you _____ to my advice in the first place, you wouldn't be in this mess right now.
      A. listen   B. will listen   C. had listened   D. listened

10. _____ interested in that subject, I would try to learn more about it.

    A. If I am   B. Should I   C. I was   D. Were I

11. If I _____ the same problems you had as a child, I might not have succeeded in life as well as you have.

    A. have   B. would have   C. had had   D. should have

12. I _____ you sooner had someone told me you were in the hospital.

    A. would have visited   C. had visited

    B. visited   D. visit

13. _____ more help, I could call my neighbor.

    A. Needed   B. Should I need   C. I have needed   D. I should need

14. _____ then what I know today, I would have saved myself a lot of time and trouble over the years.

    A. If I know   B. If I would know   C. Did I know   D. Had I known

15. Do you think there would be less conflict in the world if all people _____ the same language?

    A. speak   B. will speak   C. spoke   D. had spoken

16. If you can give me one good reason for your acting like this, _____ this incident again.

    A. I don't mention   C. I never mention

    B. I will never mention   D. will I never mention

17. I didn't know you were asleep. Otherwise, I _____ so much noise when I came in.

    A. didn't make   C. won't make

    B. wouldn't have made   D. don't make

18. Unless you _____ all of my questions, I can't do anything to help you.

    A. answered   B. answer   C. would answer   D. are answering

19. Had you told me that this was going to happen, I _____ it.

    A. would never have believed   C. hadn't believed

    B. don't believe   D. can't believe

20. If Jake _____ to go on the trip, would you have gone?

    A. doesn't agree   B. didn't agree   C. hadn't agreed   D. wouldn't agree

◇ **PRACTICE 11. Review: conditional sentences. (Charts 20-1 → 20-8)**
Directions: Complete the sentences with the words in parentheses.

1. I'm broke, but I *(have)* _____ plenty of money now if I

    (spend, not) _____ so much yesterday.

2. That child had a narrow escape. She *(hit)* _____ by a car if her

    mother *(pull, not)* _____ her out of the street.

3. A: Why were you late for the meeting?

    B: Well, I *(be)* _____ there on time, but I had a flat tire on the way.

4. A: Did you know that Bob got 100% on the test?

    B: Really? That surprises me. If I didn't know better, I *(think)* _____

        he cheated.

5. A: How did you do on the test?

    B: Not so well. I *(do)* _____ much better, but I misread the

        directions for the last section.

6. A: Do you really mean it?

    B: Of course! I *(say, not)* _____ it unless I *(mean)*

        _____ it.

7. A: When did Mark graduate?

    B: He didn't.

    A: Oh?

    B: He had to quit school because of some trouble at home. Otherwise, he *(graduate)*

        _____ last June.

8. A: I hear Dorothy had an accident. Was it serious?

    B: No. Luckily, she wasn't driving fast at the time of the accident. If she *(drive)* _____

        _____ fast, I'm sure it *(be)* _____

    a more serious accident.

9. Tom's hobby is collecting stamps from all over the world. If he *(travel)* _____

    _____ to a new country, he *(spend, always)* _____

    _____ time looking for new stamps. That's how he has acquired such a large

collection of valuable stamps.

◇ **PRACTICE 12. *As if/as though.* (Chart 20-9)**

    Directions: Using the information in parentheses, complete the sentences.

    1. Tim acts as if he ___were___ the boss. *(Truth: Tim isn't the boss.)*

    2. This hole in my shirt looks as if it ___had been made___ by a bullet. *(Truth: The hole*

        wasn't made by a bullet.)

    3. Barbara looked at me as though she _____ never _____ me before.

        (Truth: She has met me many times before.)

    4. They treat their dog as if it _____ a child. *(Truth: The dog isn't a child.)*

    5. She went right on talking as though she _____ a word I'd said.

        (Truth: She heard everything I said.)

    6. You look so depressed. You look as if you _____ a friend in the world.

        (Truth: You have many friends.)

7. He looked right through me as if I _____. (*Truth: I exist.*)

8. Craig bumped the other car and then continued as though nothing _____.
   (*Truth: Something happened.*)

9. A: Have Joe and Diane ever met?

   B: I don't think so. Why?

   A: He came in and started talking to her as if they _____ old friends.
      (*Truth: They aren't old friends.*)

10. I can hear his voice so clearly that it's as if he _____ here in this room.
    (*Truth: He isn't here in this room; he's next door.*)

11. It was so quiet that it seemed as if the earth _____. (*Truth: The earth
    didn't stop.*)

12. I turned, and there she was. It was as though she _____ out of nowhere.
    (*Truth: She didn't appear out of nowhere.*)

◇ **PRACTICE 13. Using *wish*. (Charts 20-10 and 20-11)**
   Directions: Using the information in parentheses, complete the sentences.

   1. (*The sun isn't shining.*) I wish the sun _____*were shining*_____ right now.

   2. (*I wanted you to go.*) I wish you __*had gone*__ with us to the concert last night.

   3. (*Spiro didn't drive.*) I wish Spiro _____ to work. I'd ask him for a ride
      home.

   4. (*I can't swim.*) I wish I _____ so I would feel safe in a boat.

   5. (*I want you to stop fighting.*) I wish you _____ fighting and try to work
      things out.

   6. (*I wanted to win.*) I wish we _____ the game last night.

   7. (*Bill didn't get the promotion.*) I wish Bill _____ the promotion. He feels
      bad.

   8. (*I quit my job.*) I wish I _____ my job until I'd found another one.

   9. (*It isn't winter.*) I wish it _____ winter so that I could go skiing.

   10. (*I want Al to sing.*) I wish Al _____ a couple of songs. He has a good voice.

   11. (*Natasha can't bring her children.*) I wish Natasha _____ her children
       with her tomorrow. They would be good company for mine.

   12. (*No one offered to help.*) I wish someone _____ to help us find our way
       when we got lost in the middle of the city.

Conditional Sentences and Wishes **231**

◇ **PRACTICE 14. Using *wish*. (Charts 20-10 and 20-11)**
Directions: Complete the sentences with the words in parentheses.

1. Pedro's in trouble with the teacher. Now he wishes he *(miss, not)* __hadn't missed__
   class three times this week.

2. A: It's raining. I wish it *(stop)* __would stop__.
   B: Me too. I wish the sun *(shine)* __were shining__ so that we could go swimming.

3. Heinrich doesn't like his job as a house painter. He wishes he *(go)* _____ to
   art school when he was younger. He wishes he *(can paint)* _____
   canvasses instead of houses for a living.

4. I wish I *(move, not)* _____ to this town. I can't seem to make any
   friends, and everything is so congested. I wish I *(take)* _____ the job I
   was offered in the small town near here.

5. I know I should quit smoking. I wish you *(stop)* _____ nagging me
   about it.

6. A: Did you get your car back from the garage?
   B: Yes, and it still isn't fixed. I wish I *(pay, not)* _____ them in full
   when I picked up the car. I should have waited to be sure that everything was all right.

7. A: I wish you *(hurry)* _____! We're going to be late.
   B: I wish you *(relax)* _____. We've got plenty of time.

8. I wish my husband *(invite, not)* _____ the neighbors over for dinner
   when he talked to them this afternoon. I don't feel like cooking a big dinner.

9. A: How do you like the new president of our association?
   B: Not much. I wish she *(elect, not)* _____. I never should
   have voted for her.
   A: Oh, really? Then you probably wish I *(vote, not)* _____ for her. If
   you recall, she won by only one vote. You and I could have changed the outcome of the
   election if we'd known then what we know now.

10. A: I wish we *(buy)* _____ everything we wanted all the time.
    B: In that case, you probably wish money *(grow)* _____ on trees. We'd plant
    some in the back yard, and just go out and pick a little from the branches every morning.

11. A: My thirteen-year-old daughter wishes she *(be, not)* _____ so tall and that her
    hair *(be)* _____ black and straight.
    B: Really? My daughter wishes she *(be)* _____ taller and that her hair *(be)* _____
    blond and curly.

12. A: I wish most world leaders (meet) _____ in the near future and reach
    some agreement on environmental issues. I'm worried the earth is running out of time.
    B: I wish I (disagree) _____ with you and (prove) _____
    _____ your fears groundless, but I'm afraid you might be right.

13. A: I can't go to the game with you this afternoon.
    B: Really? That's too bad. But I wish you (tell) _____ me sooner so
    that I could have found someone else to go with.

14. A: How long have you been sick?
    B: For over a week.
    A: I wish you (go) _____ to see a doctor today. You should find out
    what's wrong with you.
    B: Maybe I'll go tomorrow.

◇ **PRACTICE 15. Conditionals. (Charts 20-1 → 20-11)**
   Directions: Complete the sentences with the words in parentheses.

TOM: What's wrong, Bob? You look awful! You look as if you *(1. run)* _____
     over by a truck!

BOB: Well, you *(2. look)* _____ this bad today, too, if you *(3. have)*
     _____ a day like mine yesterday. My car slid into a tree because the
     roads were icy.

TOM: Oh? I was driving on the icy roads yesterday, and I didn't slide into a tree. What happened?

BOB: Well, I suppose if I *(4. drive, not)* _____ so fast, I *(5. slide, not)*
     _____ into the tree.

TOM: Icy roads and speed don't mix. If drivers *(6. step)* _____ on the gas on
     ice, they're likely to spin their car in a circle.

BOB: I know! And not only is my car a mess now, but I didn't have my driver's license with me,
     so now I'll have to pay an extra fine when I go to court next month.

TOM: Why were you driving without your license?

BOB: Well, I lost my wallet a few days ago. It slipped out of my pocket while I was riding the bus
     to work.

TOM: What a tale of woe! If you *(7. take not)* _____ that bus, you *(8. lose, not)*
     _____ your wallet. If you *(9. lose, not)* _____
     your wallet, you *(10. have)* _____ your driver's license with you when

you hit a tree. If you *(11. have)* _____ your license with you, you

(12. have to pay, not) _____ a big fine when you go to court

next week. And of course, if you *(13. drive, not)* _____ too

fast, you *(14. run into, not)* _____ a tree, and you *(15. be, not)*

_____ in this mess now. If I *(16. be)* _____ you, I

(17. take) _____ it easy for a while and just *(18. stay)* _____

home where you're safe and sound.

BOB: Enough about me! How about you?

TOM: Well, things are really looking up for me. I'm planning to take off for Florida as soon as I

finish my finals. I'm sick of all this cold, rainy weather we've been having. I *(19. stay)*

_____ here for vacation if the weather *(20. be, not)* _____

so bad. But I need some sun!

BOB: I wish I *(21. go)* _____ with you. How are you planning on getting

there?

TOM: If I have enough money, I *(22. fly)* _____. Otherwise, I *(23. take)*

_____ the bus. I wish I *(24. drive)* _____ my own

car there because it *(25. be)* _____ nice to have it to drive around in

once I get there, but it's such a long trip. I've been looking for a friend to go with me and

share the driving.

BOB: Hey, I have a super idea! Why don't I go with you? I can share the driving. I'm a great

driver!

TOM: Didn't you just get through telling me that you'd wrapped your car around a tree?

◇ **PRACTICE 16. TEST A: Conditional sentences. (Chapter 20)**
   Directions: Choose the correct answer.

   Example: If I ___C___ you, I would get some rest before the game tomorrow.
      A. am   B. could be   C. were   D. had been

1. When I stopped talking, Sam finished my sentence for me as though he _____ my mind.
   A. would read   B. had read   C. reads   D. can read

2. If you _____, I would have brought my friends over to your house this evening to watch
   TV, but I didn't want to bother you.
   A. had studied   C. hadn't been studying
   B. studied   D. didn't study

3. I wish I _____ you some money for your rent, but I'm broke myself.
   A. can lend   B. would lend   C. could lend   D. will lend

4. If someone _____ into the store, smile and say, "May I help you?"
   A. comes   B. came   C. would come   D. could come

5. "Are we lost?"
   "I think so. I wish we _____ a map with us today."
   A. were bringing   B. brought   C. had brought   D. would bring

6. "Here's my phone number."
   "Thanks. I'll give you a call if I _____ some help tomorrow."
   A. will need   B. need   C. would need   D. needed

7. If I weren't working for an accounting firm, I _____ in a bank.
   A. work   B. will work   C. have worked   D. would be working

8. Ed invested a lot of money with a dishonest advisor, and lost nearly all of it. Now he is
   having serious financial problems. He _____ in this position if he'd listened to some of his
   friends.
   A. will be   B. wouldn't be   C. will be   D. hadn't been

9. The world _____ a better place if we had known a hundred years ago what we know today
   about the earth's environment.
   A. will be   B. was   C. should be   D. might be

10. The medicine made me feel dizzy. I felt as though the room _____ around and around.
    A. were spinning   C. spins
    B. will spin   D. would be spinning

11. "I'm really sorry about what happened during the meeting. I felt I had no choice."
    "It's okay. I'm sure you wouldn't have done it if you _____."
    A. should have   B. had to   C. hadn't had to   D. have to

12. _____ you, I'd think twice about that decision. It could be a bad move.
    A. If I had been   B. Were I   C. Should I be   D. If I am

13. "Was Pam seriously injured in the automobile accident?"
    "She broke her arm. It _____ much worse if she hadn't been wearing her seat belt."
    A. will be   B. would have been   C. was   D. were

14. If my candidate had won the election, I _____ happy now.

    A. am   B. would be   C. was   D. can be

15. I wish Janet _____ to the meeting this afternoon.

    A. came   B. will come   C. can come   D. could come

16. I _____ you to the woman I was speaking with, but I couldn't think of her name.

    A. will introduce   C. would have introduced

    B. would introduce   D. couldn't have introduced

17. "What _____ today if you hadn't come here this weekend?"

    "I guess I'd be putting in extra hours at my office."

    A. are you doing   C. will you be doing

    B. can you do   D. would you be doing

18. Page 12 of the manual that came with the appliance says, "_____ any problem with the merchandise, contact your local dealer."

    A. Do you have   C. Had you

    B. Should you have   D. You have

19. Marge walked away from the discussion. Otherwise, she _____ something she would regret later.

    A. will say   B. said   C. might say   D. might have said

20. I would never have encouraged you to go into this field _____ it would be so stressful for you. I'm sorry it's been so difficult for you.

    A. had I known   C. should I know

    B. and I have known   D. but I knew

◇ **PRACTICE 17. TEST B: Conditional sentences. (Chapter 20)**
Directions: Choose the correct answer.

Example: If I __C__ you, I would get some rest before the game tomorrow.
    A. am   B. could be   C. were   D. had been

1. Please keep your voice down in this section of the library. If you _____ to talk loudly, I will have to ask you to leave.
    A. continued   B. could continue   C. will continue   D. continue

2. Gloria never seems to get tired. I sure wish I _____ her energy.
    A. would have   B. have   C. have had   D. had

3. "Why didn't Bill get the promotion he was expecting?"
   "He may not be qualified. If he were, he _____ that promotion last year."
    A. would have been given   C. would be given
    B. was given   D. had been given

4. If I could find Rob's phone number, I _____ him about the change in plans. Maybe somebody else will call him.
    A. called   B. had called   C. could call   D. will call

5. "How do you like your new apartment?"
   "The apartment itself is great, but I wish I _____ used to the constant noise from the street below."
    A. got   B. could get   C. had gotten   D. am

6. I was very engrossed in that presentation on Australia. The videotapes were so realistic that it was as though we _____ there, driving through the outback.
    A. were   B. have been   C. are   D. will be

7. If I _____ following that other car too closely, I would have been able to stop in time instead of running into it.
    A. wasn't   B. would have been   C. was   D. hadn't been

8. "Why aren't you going mountain climbing with the rest of us next weekend?"
   "To be honest with you, I'm lazy. If I weren't, I _____ with you."
    A. would have gone   C. go
    B. would go   D. will go

9. "Will you see Tom at lunch today? I'd like you to give him a message for me."
   "I'm not going to lunch, but if I _____ him later, I'll give him your message."
    A. should see   B. will see   C. would see   D. could see

10. I'm really sleepy today. I wish I _____ Bob to the airport late last night.
    A. didn't have to take   C. hadn't had to take
    B. weren't taking   D. didn't take

11. Hurry! We've got to leave the house immediately. Otherwise, _____ the opening ceremony.
    A. we'd miss   C. we miss
    B. we'd have missed   D. we're going to miss

12. "Why didn't you tell me you were having so many problems?"
    "I _____ you, but I figured you had enough to worry about without my problems, so I said nothing."
    A. would tell   B. would have told   C. would be telling   D. had told

13. A nation's balance of trade is considered unfavorable if it _____ more money on imports than it gains from exports.
    A. will spend   B. would spend   C. can spend   D. spends

14. Many people who live near nuclear plants are concerned. _____ go wrong, the impact on the surrounding area could be disastrous.
    A. Something would   C. Should something
    B. Something will   D. Does something

15. Had I known the carpenter was going to take three days to show up, I _____ the materials and done the work myself. It would be finished by now.
    A. will get   C. might get
    B. would have gotten   D. will have gotten

16. I wish you _____ making that noise. It's bothering me.
    A. would stop   C. stop
    B. are going to stop   D. can stop

17. A huge tree crashed through the bedroom roof and broke my bed and most of the other furniture. _____ in the room, I would have been killed.
    A. Should I be   C. Would I have been
    B. Had I been   D. Would I be

18. If everyone _____, how would we control air traffic? Surely, we'd all be crashing into each other.
    A. can fly   B. will fly   C. flies   D. could fly

19. If the world's tropical forests continue to disappear at their present rate, many animal species _____ extinct.
    A. became   C. will become
    B. would have become   D. would become

20. When my lost briefcase was returned with my year-long research results intact, I felt tremendously relieved. It was as if a huge, heavy weight _____ from my shoulders.
    A. had been lifted   C. would be lifted
    B. is being lifted   D. is lifting

APPENDIX
Supplementary Grammar Units

◇ **PRACTICE 1. Subjects, verbs, and objects. (Chart A-1)**
Directions: <u>Underline</u> and identify the subject (S), verb (V), and object of the verb (O) in each sentence.

             S   V   O
1. <u>Airplanes</u> <u>have</u> <u>wings</u>.

2. The teacher explained the problem.

3. Children enjoy games.

4. Jack wore a blue suit.

5. Some animals eat plants. Some animals eat other animals.

6. According to an experienced waitress, you can carry full cups of coffee without spilling them just by never looking at them.

◇ **PRACTICE 2. Transitive vs. intransitive verbs. (Chart A-1)**
Directions: <u>Underline</u> and identify the verb in each sentence. Write **VT** if it is transitive. Write **VI** if it is intransitive.

           VI
1. Alice <u>arrived</u> at six o'clock.

        VT
2. We <u>drank</u> some tea.

3. I agree with you.

4. I waited for Sam at the airport for two hours.

5. They're staying at a resort hotel in San Antonio, Texas.

6. Chanchai is studying English.

7. The wind is blowing hard today.

8. I walked to the theater, but Janice rode her bicycle.

9. Amphibians hatch from eggs.

10. Rivers flow toward the sea.

◇ **PRACTICE 3. Identifying prepositions. (Chart A-2)**
Directions: <u>Underline</u> the prepositions.

1. Jim came to class <u>without</u> his books.

2. We stayed at home during the storm.

3. Sonya walked across the bridge over the Cedar River.

4. When Alex walked through the door, his little sister ran toward him and put her arms around his neck.

5. The two of us need to talk to Tom, too.

6. Animals live in all parts of the world. Animals walk or crawl on land, fly in the air, and swim in the water.

7. Scientists divide living things into two main groups: the animal kingdom and the plant kingdom.

8. Asia extends from the Pacific Ocean in the east to Africa and Europe in the west.

◇ **PRACTICE 4. Sentence elements. (Charts A-1 and A-2)**
Directions: <u>Underline</u> and identify the subject (**S**), verb (**V**) object (**O**), and prepositional phrases (**PP**) in the following sentences.

       S   **V**   **O**   **PP**
1. <u>Jack</u> <u>put</u> the <u>letter</u> <u>in the mailbox</u>.

2. The children walked to school.

3. Mary did her homework at the library.

4. Chinese printers created the first paper money in the world.

5. Dark clouds appeared on the horizon.

6. Mary filled the shelves of the cabinet with boxes of old books.

◇ **PRACTICE 5. Adjectives and adverbs. (Charts A-3 and A-4)**
Directions: <u>Underline</u> and identify the adjectives (**ADJ**) and adverbs (**ADV**) in these sentences.

            ADJ   **ADV**
1. Jack opened the <u>heavy</u> door <u>slowly</u>.

2. Chinese jewelers carved beautiful ornaments from jade.

3. The old man carves wooden figures skillfully.

4. A busy executive usually has short conversations on the telephone.

5. The young woman had a very good time at the picnic yesterday.

◇ **PRACTICE 6. Adjectives and adverbs. (Charts A-3 and A-4)**
Directions: Complete each sentence with the correct adjective or adverb.

1. *quick, quickly*   We ate ___quickly___ and ran to the theater.

2. *quick, quickly*   We had a ___quick___ dinner and ran to the theater.

3. *polite, politely*   I've always found Fred to be a _____ person.

4. *polite, politely*   He responded to my question _____ .

5. *regular, regularly*   Mr. Thomas comes to the store _____ for cheese and bread.

6. *regular, regularly*   He is a _____ customer.

7. *usual, usually*   The teacher arrived at the _____ time.

8. *usual, usually*   She _____ comes to class five minutes before it begins.

9. *good, well*   Jennifer Cooper paints _____ .

10. *good, well*   She is a _____ artist.

11. *gentle, gently*   A _____ breeze touched my face.

12. *gentle, gently*   A breeze _____ touched my face.

13. *annual, annually*   Many birds migrate _____ to a warm climate for the winter.

14. *annual, annually*   Many birds fly long distances in their _____ migration to a warm climate for the winter.

15. *bad, badly*   The audience booed the actors' _____ performance.

16. *bad, badly*   The audience booed and whistled because the actors performed _____ throughout the show.

◇ **PRACTICE 7. Midsentence adverbs. (Chart A-4)**
Directions: Put the adverb in parentheses in its usual midsentence position.

1. *(always)*   Sue ∧ takes a walk in the morning.
              always

2. *(always)*   Tim is a hard worker.

3. *(always)*   Beth has worked hard.

4. *(always)*   Jack works hard.

5. *(always)*   Do you work hard?

6. *(usually)*   Taxis are available at the airport.

7. *(rarely)*   Youssef takes a taxi to his office.

8. *(often)*   I have thought about quitting my job and sailing to Alaska.

9. *(probably)*   Yuko needs some help.

10. *(ever)*   Have you attended the show at the planetarium?

11. *(seldom)*   Al goes out to eat at a restaurant.

12. *(hardly ever)*   The students are late.

13. *(usually)*   Do you finish your homework before dinner?

14. *(generally)*   In India, the monsoon season begins in April.

15. *(usually)*   During the monsoon season, Mr. Singh's hometown receives around

                         610 centimeters (240 inches) of rain, which is an unusually large amount.

◇ **PRACTICE 8. Linking verbs. (Charts A-1 → A-6)**
Directions: Some of the *italicized* words in the following are used as linking verbs. Identify which ones are linking verbs by <u>underlining</u> them. Also underline the adjective that follows the linking verb.

1. Olga *looked* at the fruit. *(no underline)*

2. It <u>*looked*</u> <u>fresh</u>.

3. Dan *noticed* a scratch on the door of his car.

4. Morris *tasted* the candy.

5. It *tasted* good.

6. The crowd *grew* quiet as the official began her speech.

7. Felix *grows* tomatoes in his garden.

8. Sally *grew* up in Florida.

9. I can *smell* the chicken in the oven.

10. It *smells* delicious.

11. Barbara *got* a package in the mail.

12. Al *got* sleepy after dinner.

13. During the storm, the sea *became* rough.

14. Nicole *became* a doctor after many years of study.

15. Diana *sounded* her horn to warn the driver of the other car.

16. Helen *sounded* happy when I talked to her.

17. The weather *turns* hot in July.

18. When Bob entered the room, I *turned* around to look at him.

19. I *turned* a page in the book.

20. It *appears* certain that Mary Hanson will win the election.

21. Dick's story *seems* strange. Do you believe it?

◇ **PRACTICE 9. Linking verbs; adjectives and adverbs. (Charts A-3 → A-6)**
Directions: Complete each sentence with the correct adjective or adverb.

1. *clean, cleanly*   The floor looks ___clean___ .

2. *slow, slowly*   The bear climbed ___slowly___ up the tree.

3. *safe, safely*   The plane landed _____ on the runway.

4. *anxious, anxiously*   When the wind started to blow, I grew _____ .

5. *complete, completely*   This list of names appears _____ . No more names need to be added.

6. *wild, wildly*   The crowd yelled _____ when we scored a goal.

7. *honest, honestly*   The merchant looked _____ , but she wasn't. I discovered when I got home that she had cheated me.

8. *thoughtful, thoughtfully* Jane looked at her book _____ before she answered the teacher's question.

9. *good, well*   Most of the students did _____ on their tests.

10. *fair, fairly*   The contract offer sounded _____ to me, so I accepted the job.

11. *terrible, terribly*   Jim felt _____ about forgetting his son's birthday.

12. *good, well*   A rose smells _____ .

13. *light, lightly*   As dawn approached, the sky became _____ .

14. *confident, confidently* Beth spoke _____ when she delivered her speech.

15. *famous, famously*   The actor became _____ throughout much of the world.

16. *fine, finely*   I don't think this milk is spoiled. It tastes _____ to me.

◇ **PRACTICE 10. Review: basic question forms. (Chart B-1)**
> *Directions:* From the <u>underlined</u> sentences, make questions for the given answers. Fill in the blank spaces with the appropriate words. If no word is needed, write **Ø**.

1. <u>**Bob can live there**</u>.

	Question word	Auxiliary verb	Subject	Main verb	Rest of question	→	Answer
1a.	Ø	Can	Bob	live	there	? →	Yes.
1b.	Where	can	Bob	live	Ø	? →	There.
1c.	Who	can	Ø	live	there	? →	Bob.

2. <u>**Don is living there**</u>.

	Question word	Auxiliary verb	Subject	Main verb	Rest of question	→	Answer
2a.	Ø				there	? →	Yes.
2b.	Where				Ø	? →	There.
2c.	Who				there	? →	Don.

3. <u>**Sue lives there**</u>.

	Question word	Auxiliary verb	Subject	Main verb	Rest of question	→	Answer
3a.	Ø				there	? →	Yes.
3b.	Where				Ø	? →	There.
3c.	Who				there	? →	Sue.

4. <u>**Ann will live there**</u>.

	Question word	Auxiliary verb	Subject	Main verb	Rest of question	→	Answer
4a.	Ø				there	? →	Yes.
4b.	Where				Ø	? →	There.
4c.	Who				there	? →	Ann.

5. <u>**Jack lived there**</u>.

	Question word	Auxiliary verb	Subject	Main verb	Rest of question	→	Answer
5a.					there	? →	Yes.
5b.					Ø	? →	There.
5c.					there	? →	Jack.

6. <u>**Mary has lived there**</u>.

	Question word	Auxiliary verb	Subject	Main verb	Rest of question	→	Answer
6a.						? →	Yes.
6b.						? →	There.
6c.						? →	Mary.

◇ **PRACTICE 11. Yes/no and information questions. (Charts B-1 and B-2)**
Directions: Create questions to fit the dialogues. There are two speakers in each dialogue: A and B. Notice in the examples that in each dialogue there is a short answer and then in parentheses a long answer. Your questions should produce those answers.

1. A: _____When are you going to the zoo?_____
   B: Tomorrow. *(I'm going to the zoo tomorrow.)*

2. A: _____Are you going downtown later today?_____
   B: Yes. *(I'm going downtown later today.)*

3. A: _____
   B: Yes. *(I live in an apartment.)*

4. A: _____
   B: In a condominium. *(Sue lives in a condominium.)*

5. A: _____
   B: Jack. *(Jack lives in that house.)*

6. A: _____
   B: Yes. *(I can speak French.)*

7. A: _____
   B: Don. *(Don can speak Arabic.)*

8. A: _____
   B: Two weeks ago. *(Olga arrived two weeks ago.)*

9. A: _____
   B: Ali. *(Ali arrived late.)*

10. A: _____
    B: The window. *(Ann is opening the window.)*

11. A: _____
    B: Opening the window. *(Ann is opening the window.)*

12. A: _____
    B: Her book. *(Mary opened her book.)*

13. A: _____
    B: Tom. *(Tom opened the door.)*

14. A: _____
    B: Yes. *(The mail has arrived.)*

15. A: _____
    B: Yes. *(I have a bicycle.)*

16. A: _____
    B: A pen. *(Alex has a pen in his hand.)*

17. A: _____

    B: Yes. (*I like ice cream.*)

18. A: _____

    B: Yes. (*I would like an ice cream cone.*)

19. A: _____

    B: A candy bar. (*Joe would like a candy bar.*)

20. A: _____

    B: Ann. (*Ann would like a soft drink.*)

◇ **PRACTICE 12. Yes/no and information questions. (Charts B-1 and B-2)**
Directions: Create questions to fit the dialogues. There are two speakers in each dialogue: A and B. Notice in the examples that in each dialogue there is a short answer and then in parentheses a long answer. Your questions should produce those answers.

1. A: _____How long has Pierre been living here?_____

    B: Since last September. (*Pierre has been living here since last September.*)

2. A: I need some information. Maybe you can help me. ____Which (city) is farther_____
    ____north, London or Paris?_____

    B: London. (*London is farther north than Paris.*)

3. A: Is that your umbrella?

    B: No.

    A: _____

    B: Jane's. (*It's Jane's.*)

4. A: I haven't seen you for weeks. How are you? _____

    B: Going to school and studying hard. (*I've been going to school and studying hard.*)

5. A: Did you call Sally?

    B: Yes, but she wasn't in.

    A: _____

    B: Her roommate. (*Her roommate answered the phone.*)

6. A: Do the villagers have tractors in the rural areas?

    B: No. They don't have any modern farm machinery.

    A: _____

    B: With oxen or water buffaloes. (*They plow their fields with oxen or water buffaloes.*)

7. A: I really like having my own computer.

    B: _____

    A: Since last December. (*I've had it since last December.*)

8. A: _____ I've never seen one quite like it.

   B: A myna. It's common in warm climates. *(That kind of bird is a myna.)*

9. A: _____

   B: I missed my bus. *(I was late for work this morning because I missed my bus.)*

10. A: Last summer we painted the outside of our house.

    B: That must have been a big job. _____

    A: About four days. *(It took about four days.)*

11. A: Jack was late last night, wasn't he? _____

    B: At 11:30. *(He finally got home at 11:30.)*

12. A: Would you like a cup of coffee?

    B: Thanks. That sounds good.

    A: _____

    B: With cream and sugar. *(I take it with cream and sugar.)*

13. A: _____

    B: Around 250 million. *(The population of the United States is around 250 million.)*

14. A: _____

    B: The red one. *(Of those two coats, I like the red one better than the black one.)*

15. A: We spent a relaxing weekend in a small village in the mountains.

    B: _____

    A: By bus. *(We got there by bus.)*

16. A: I'm sending a letter to the consulate about the problems I'm having with my visa.

    _____

    B: Mr. Ho. *(You should address it to Mr. Ho.)*

17. A: _____

    B: Over 800 miles. *(It's over 800 miles from here to Los Angeles.)*

18. A: _____

    B: Ann, Susan, and Alice. *(Ann, Susan, and Alice are going to be at the meeting tonight.)*

19. A: In my country, we eat rice every day. _____

    B: About once a week. *(People in my country have rice about once a week.)*

20. A: _____

    B: Silly looking hat?! I think it's a great hat! I got it at the shopping mall. *(I got that silly looking hat at the shopping mall.)*

21. A: _____

    B: To say you're sorry. *(Apologize means "to say you're sorry.")*

22. A: _____

    B: Twelve. *(There are twelve edges on a cube.)*

    A: _____

    B: Eight. *(There are eight edges on a pyramid.)*

23. A: I've never met Bob. _____

    B: *He has dark hair, a mustache, wears glasses, and is about average height.*

24. A: You know Ann Green, don't you? _____

    B: *She's energetic, bright, very friendly. A really nice person.*

◇ **PRACTICE 13. Information questions. (Charts B-1 and B-2)**

Directions: Create questions from these sentences. The *italicized* words in parentheses should be the answers to your questions.

1. I take my coffee *(black)*. → *How do you take your coffee?*

2. I have *(an English-Spanish)* dictionary.

3. He *(runs a grocery store)* for a living.

4. Margaret was talking to *(her uncle)*.

5. *(Only ten)* people showed up for the meeting.

6. *(Due to heavy fog)*, none of the planes could take off.

7. She was thinking about *(her experiences as a rural doctor)*.

8. I was driving *(sixty-five miles per hour)* when the policeman stopped me.

9. I like *(hot and spicy Mexican)* food best.

10. *(The)* apartment *(at the end of the hall on the second floor)* is mine.

11. Oscar is *(friendly, generous, and kindhearted)*.

12. Oscar is *(tall and thin and has short black hair)*.

13. *(Ann's)* dictionary fell to the floor.

14. Abby isn't here *(because she has a doctor's appointment)*.

15. All of the students in the class will be informed of their final grades *(on Friday)*.

16. I feel *(awful)*.

17. Of those three books, I preferred *(the one by Tolstoy)*.

18. I like *(rock)* music.

19. The plane is expected to be *(an hour)* late.

20. The driver of the stalled car lit a flare *(in order to warn oncoming cars)*.

21. I want *(the felt-tip)* pen, *(not the ballpoint)*.

22. The weather is *(hot and humid)* in July.

23. I like my steak *(medium rare)*.

24. I did *(very well)* on the test.

25. There are *(31,536,000)* seconds in a year.

◇ **PRACTICE 14. Information questions. (Charts B-1 and B-2)**
   Directions: Create questions from the following sentences. The words in parentheses should be the answers to your questions.

   1. I need *(five dollars)*. → *How much money do you need?*

   2. Roberto was born *(in Panama)*.

   3. I go out to eat *(at least once a week)*.

   4. I'm waiting for *(Maria)*.

   5. *(My sister)* answered the phone.

   6. I called *(Benjamin)*.

   7. *(Benjamin)* called.

   8. She bought *(twelve gallons of)* gas.

   9. "Deceitful" means *("dishonest")*.

   10. An abyss is *(a bottomless hole)*.

   11. He went *(this)* way, *(not that way)*.

   12. These are *(Jim's)* books and papers.

   13. They have *(four)* children.

   14. He has been here *(for two hours)*.

   15. It is *(two hundred miles)* to New Orleans.

   16. The doctor can see you *(at three on Friday)*.

   17. Her roommate is *(Jane Peters)*.

   18. Her roommates are *(Jane Peters and Sue Lee)*.

   19. My parents have been living there *(for three years)*.

   20. This is *(Alice's)* book.

   21. *(Fred and Jack)* are coming over for dinner.

   22. Ann's dress is *(blue)*.

   23. Anne's eyes are *(brown)*.

   24. *(Bob)* can't go on the picnic.

   25. Bob can't go *(because he is sick)*.

   26. I didn't answer the phone *(because I didn't hear it ring)*.

   27. I like *(classical)* music.

   28. I don't understand *(the chart on page 50)*.

29. Janet is *(studying)* right now.

30. You spell "sitting" *(with two "t's" S-I-T-T-I-N-G)*.

31. Tom *(is about medium height and has red hair and freckles)*.

32. Tom is *(very serious and hardworking)*.

33. Ron *(works as a civil engineer for the railroad company)*.

34. Mexico is *(eight hundred miles)* from here.

35. I take my coffee *(black with sugar)*.

36. Of Stockholm and Moscow, *(Stockholm)* is farther north.

37. *(Fine.)* I'm getting along *(just fine)*.

◇ **PRACTICE 15. Negative questions. (Chart B-4)**
   Directions: In these dialogues, make negative questions from the words in parentheses, and determine the expected response.

1. A: Your infected finger looks terrible. *(you, see, not)* ___Haven't you seen___ a doctor yet?

   B: ___No___ . But I'm going to. I don't want the infection to get any worse.

2. A: You look pale. What's the matter? *(you, feel)* _____ well?

   B: _____ . I think I might be coming down with something.

3. A: Did you see Mark at the meeting?

   B: No, I didn't.

   A: Really? *(he, be, not)* _____ there?

   B: _____ .

   A: That's funny. I've never known him to miss a meeting before.

4. A: Why didn't you come to the meeting yesterday afternoon?

   B: What meeting? I didn't know there was a meeting.

   A: *(Mary, tell, not)* _____ you about it?

   B: _____ . No one said a word to me about it.

5. A: I have a package for Janet. *(Janet and you, work, not)* _____
   _____ in the same building?

   B: _____ . I'd be happy to take the package to her tomorrow when I go to work.

6. A: Frank didn't report all of his income on his tax forms.

   B: *(that, be, not)* _____ against the law?

   A: _____ . And that's why he's in a lot of legal trouble. He might even go to jail.

7. A: Did you give Linda my message when you went to class this morning?

   B: No. I didn't see her.

   A: Oh? *(she, be)* _____ in class?

   B: _____ . She didn't come today.

8. A: Do you see that woman over there, the one in the blue dress? *(she, be)* _____

   Mrs. Robbins?

   B: _____ .

   A: I thought so. I wonder what she is doing here.

◇ **PRACTICE 16. Tag questions. (Chart B-5)**
  Directions: Add tag questions to the following.

   1. You live in an apartment, _don't you_ ?

   2. You've never been in Italy, _have you_ ?

   3. Sally turned in her report, _____ ?

   4. There are more countries north of the equator than south of it, _____ ?

   5. You've never met Jack Freeman, _____ ?

   6. You have a ticket to the game, _____ ?

   7. You'll be there, _____ ?

   8. Tom knows Alice Reed, _____ ?

   9. We should call Rita, _____ ?

  10. Ostriches can't swim, _____ ?

  11. These books aren't yours, _____ ?

  12. That's Bob's, _____ ?

  13. No one died in the accident, _____ ?

  14. I'm right, _____ ?

  15. This grammar is easy, _____ ?

◇ **PRACTICE 17. Contractions. (Chart C)**
  Directions: Write the contraction of the pronoun and verb if appropriate. Write Ø if the pronoun and verb cannot be contracted.

   1. He is (_He's_) in my class.

   2. He was (_Ø_) in my class.

   3. He has (_He's_) been here since July.

   4. He has (_Ø_) a Volvo.*

   _____

   *NOTE: ***has, have*** and ***had*** are NOT contracted when they are used as main verbs. They are contracted only
   when they are used as helping verbs.

5. She had (_____) been there for a long time before we arrived.

6. She had (_____) a bad cold.

7. She would (_____) like to go to the zoo.

8. I did (_____) well on the test.

9. We will (_____) be there early.

10. They are (_____) in their seats over there.*

11. It is (_____) going to be hot tomorrow.

12. It has (_____) been a long time since I've seen him.

13. A bear is a large animal. It has (_____) four legs and brown hair.

14. We were (_____) on time.

15. We are (_____) always on time.

16. She has (_____) a good job.

17. She has (_____) been working there for a long time.

18. She had (_____) opened the window before class began.

19. She would (_____) have helped us if we had (_____) asked her.

20. He could (_____) have helped us if he had (_____) been there.

◇ **PRACTICE 18. Using *not* and *no*. (Chart D-1)**
Directions: Change each sentence into the negative in two ways: use ***not . . . any*** in one sentence and ***no*** in the other.

1. I have some problems. → *I don't have any problems. I have no problems.*

2. There was some food on the shelf.

3. I received some letters from home.

4. I need some help.

5. We have some time to waste.

6. You should have given the beggar some money.

7. I trust someone. → *I don't trust anyone. I trust no one.***

8. I saw someone.

9. There was someone in his room.

10. She can find somebody who knows about it.

—————

*__They're, their,__ and __there__ all have the same pronunciation.
**Also spelled with a hyphen in British English: *no-one*

◇ PRACTICE 19. Avoiding double negatives. (Chart D-2)

Directions: Correct the errors in these sentences, all of which contain double negatives.

1. We don't have no time to waste.

   → *We have no time to waste.* OR: *We don't have any time to waste.*

2. I didn't have no problems.

3. I can't do nothing about it.

4. You can't hardly ever understand her when she speaks.

5. I don't know neither Ann nor her husband.

6. Don't never drink water from that river without boiling it first.

7. Because I had to sit in the back row of the auditorium, I couldn't barely hear the speaker.

◇ PRACTICE 20. Beginning a sentence with a negative word. (Chart D-3)

Directions: Change each sentence so that it begins with a negative word.

1. I had hardly stepped out of bed when the phone rang.

   → *Hardly had I stepped out of bed when the phone rang.*

2. I will never say that again.

3. I have scarcely ever enjoyed myself more than I did yesterday.

4. She rarely makes a mistake.

5. I will never trust him again because he lied to me.

6. It is hardly ever possible to get an appointment to see him.

7. I seldom skip breakfast.

8. I have never known a more generous person than Samantha.

◇ PRACTICE 21. Preposition combinations. (Chart E)

Directions: Complete the sentences with prepositions.

1. There is no excuse ___for___ lying to your friends.

2. The children are excited _____ their upcoming trip to the zoo.

3. I wasn't aware _____ any problems with the new design.

4. Are you satisfied _____ your accommodations?

5. Cubs are protected _____ danger by the mother bear.

6. Registration for the conference is limited _____ 300 participants.

7. I'm very fond _____ my nieces and nephews.

8. Do you regularly contribute _____ worthwhile causes?

9. We thanked the contributors _____ their donations.

10. The famous actor gladly answers questions that are relevant _____ her work.

11. She does not respond _____ questions about her personal life.

12. I am envious _____ no one.

13. Did Sara apologize _____ being late?

14. Lemonade is composed _____ lemon juice, water, and sugar.

15. Our apartment is furnished _____ kitchen appliances, but not a washer and dryer.

◇ **PRACTICE 22. Preposition combinations. (Chart E)**
Directions: Complete the sentences with prepositions.

1. It's important to believe _____ yourself.

2. Would you be willing to fight _____ your ideals?

3. The spy was involved _____ a dangerous conspiracy.

4. For many people it's difficult to distinguish a dolphin _____ a porpoise.

5. Gandhi was committed _____ nonviolence.

6. He will be remembered throughout the ages _____ his commitment to nonviolence.

7. If you're done _____ your dictionary, could I borrow it for a minute?

8. Usually people will be polite _____ you if you are polite _____ them.

9. Oliver is grateful _____ his parents _____ giving him the opportunity for a good education.

10. Many people are very concerned _____ global warming.

11. It took Natasha almost a year to recover _____ her automobile accident.

12. The driver of the other car was accused _____ reckless driving.

13. I do not agree _____ your political views.

14. I refuse to argue _____ you _____ politics ever again.

15. My mother introduced me _____ classical music when I was quite young.

◇ **PRACTICE 23. Preposition combinations. (Chart E)**
Directions: Complete the sentences with prepositions.

1. Susan took advantage _____ having a roommate from Chile by practicing speaking Spanish with her as often as she could.

2. The president is innocent _____ the charges leveled against him by his political opponents.

3. Under what circumstances, if any, would you be capable _____ killing another human being?

4. There is no substitute _____ good home cooking.

5. Showing that he was faithful _____ his campaign promises, the governor approved the building of ten new schools.

6. After studying the evidence, I am convinced _____ his innocence.

7. So you subscribe _____ the theory that the universe began as a Big Bang?

8. I'd like to get a high-paying job, but I'm not qualified _____ much of anything. Maybe I'd better go back to school.

9. If you need me, I'll be there. You can count _____ me.

10. The brave firefighter rescued two small children _____ a burning building.

11. A locked gate prevented us _____ entering the park.

12. The bride wore white, and the bridesmaids were dressed _____ yellow silk.

13. Ms. Fields' office is cluttered _____ stacks and stacks of papers.

14. New computers are equipped _____ all sorts of things I don't understand and never use.

15. Professor Armsley was invited to participate _____ a panel discussion on the role of business in protecting the environment.

◇ **PRACTICE 24. Preposition combinations. (Chart E)**
   Directions: Complete the sentences with prepositions.

1. Would you approve _____ a law allowing 13-year-olds to drive?

2. I myself would be opposed _____ such a law.

3. Olga's heart was filled _____ happiness on her wedding day.

4. Please don't be upset _____ me. I didn't mean to hurt your feelings.

5. Would you be interested _____ joining a hiking club?

6. I know little about the ancient Greek philosophers. I'm not acquainted _____ the works of Plato.

7. Anna, who works twelve-hour days, is dedicated _____ her research into possible cures for cancer.

8. While we're all hoping _____ better weather, we don't expect it.

9. The nightly news on TV exposes watchers _____ acts of violence that leave them fearful and horrified.

10. Sam can't keep any secrets _____ his wife. Sometimes he even feels that she knows what he's thinking.

11. My uncle stopped my cousin _____ marrying the man she loves.

12. Larry started with one small store and now has twenty stores. He has succeeded _____ business.

13. Are you complaining _____ the neighbors' children again? Maybe we should move to another apartment.

14. Are you related _____ anyone famous?

15. Mr. Adams tried to hide his gambling losses _____ his wife, but she found out.

◇ **PRACTICE 25. Preposition combinations. (Chart E)**
Directions: Complete the sentences with prepositions.

1. Would you vote _____ a woman to lead your country?

2. Stop staring _____ me! What are you doing? Is something wrong?

3. Mrs. Jefferson is known _____ her sharp intellect.

4. I look forward _____ meeting your parents.

5. The city of Kigali is located _____ Ruwanda.

6. This sentence consists _____ six words.

7. We are blessed _____ three healthy, happy, rambunctious children.

8. If you can't depend _____ your family to help you in times of trouble, who can you rely _____ ?

9. Don't blame other people _____ your own failures in life.

10. We have a date for tomorrow evening. You haven't forgotten _____ it, have you?

11. I think it's important to become familiar _____ cultures and customs different from our own.

12. We barely escaped _____ the war-torn country with our lives.

13. Do you believe that children should never be allowed to argue _____ adults _____ anything?

14. Your doctor can provide you _____ information about any health concerns you might have. Be sure to ask questions.

15. Some countries try to prohibit their citizens _____ traveling abroad.

◇ **PRACTICE 26. Preposition combinations. (Chart E)**
  Directions: Complete the sentences with prepositions.

  1. My boss demanded to know why I was absent _____ work last Friday.

  2. My neighbor takes care _____ my two children while I'm at work.

  3. At first it was hard to leave my children with a babysitter, but now I'm used _____ it.

  4. As a last resort, I covered my face _____ a scarf to keep the flies away.

  5. I applied _____ several companies _____ positions in their accounting department.

  6. As soon as I was finished _____ my dessert, we paid the bill and left the restaurant.

  7. Please forgive me _____ not getting back to you sooner.

  8. Who is responsible _____ ordering supplies in the mail room?

  9. We arrived _____ Paris around noon, but we didn't arrive _____ our friends' apartment until well after three.

  10. I'm not accustomed _____ drinking coffee. I'm a tea drinker.

  11. Siblings are often jealous _____ each other, but these jealousies usually decrease as the children mature.

  12. I'm exhausted _____ all the hard work of the past week.

  13. Would you object _____ watching a different station for the news tonight?

  14. Please be patient _____ me. I'm trying very hard to understand what you're saying, but your meaning isn't clear to me yet.

  15. It is good to be pleased _____ ourselves and proud _____ ourselves when we have done a good job.

SPECIAL WORKBOOK SECTION
Phrasal Verbs

PHRASAL VERBS (TWO-WORD AND THREE-WORD VERBS)
    The term *phrasal verb* refers to a verb and particle which together have a special meaning. For example, **put + off** means "postpone." Sometimes a phrasal verb consists of three parts. For example, **put + up + with** means "tolerate." Phrasal verbs are also called *two-word verbs* or *three-word verbs*.

SEPARABLE PHRASAL VERBS (a) *I handed* my paper *in* yesterday. (b) *I handed in* my paper yesterday. (c) *I handed* it *in* yesterday. (*INCORRECT:* I *handed in* it yesterday.)	A phrasal verb may be either *separable* or *nonseparable*. With a separable phrasal verb, a noun may come either between the verb and the preposition or after the preposition, as in (a) and (b). A pronoun comes between the verb and the preposition if the phrasal verb is separable, as in (c).

NONSEPARABLE PHRASAL VERBS
(d) *I ran into* an old friend yesterday.
(e) *I ran into* her yesterday.
    (*INCORRECT:* I *ran* an old friend *into*.)
    (*INCORRECT:* I *ran* her *into* yesterday.)
	With a nonseparable phrasal verb, a noun or pronoun must follow the preposition, as in (d) and (e).

    Phrasal verbs are especially common in informal English. Following is a list of common phrasal verbs and their usual meanings. This list contains only those phrasal verbs used in the exercises in the text. The phrasal verbs marked with an asterisk (★) are nonseparable.

A   ask out . . . . *ask someone to go on a date*

B   bring about, bring on . . . . *cause*
       bring up . . . . *(1) rear children; (2) mention or introduce a topic*

C   call back . . . . *return a telephone call*
       call in . . . . *ask to come to an official place for a specific purpose*
       call off . . . . *cancel*
       ★call on . . . . *(1) ask to speak in class; (2) visit*
       call up . . . . *call on the telephone*
       ★catch up (with) . . . . *reach the same position or level*
       ★check in, check into . . . . *register at a hotel*
       ★check into . . . . *investigate*
       ★check out . . . . *(1) take a book from the library; (2) investigate*
       ★check out (of) . . . . *leave a hotel*
       cheer up . . . . *make (someone) feel happier*
       clean up . . . . *make clean and orderly*
       ★come across . . . . *meet/find by chance*
       cross out . . . . *draw a line through*
       cut out . . . . *stop an annoying activity*

D do over . . . . *do again*
    *drop by, drop in (on) . . . . *visit informally*
    drop off . . . . *leave something/someone at a place*
    *drop out (of) . . . . *stop going to school, to a class, to a club, etc.*

F figure out . . . . *find the answer by reasoning*
    fill out . . . . *write the answers to a questionnaire or complete an official form*
    find out . . . . *discover information*

G *get along (with) . . . . *exist satisfactorily*
    get back (from) . . . . *(1) return from a place; (2) receive again*
    *get in, get into . . . . *(1) enter a car; (2) arrive*
    *get off . . . . *leave an airplane, a bus, a train, a subway, a bicycle*
    *get on . . . . *enter an airplane, a bus, a train, a subway, a bicycle*
    *get out of . . . . *(1) leave a car; (2) avoid work or an unpleasant activity*
    *get over . . . . *recover from an illness*
    *get through (with) . . . . *finish*
    *get up (from) . . . . *arise from a bed, a chair*
    give back . . . . *return an item to someone*
    give up . . . . *stop trying*
    *go over . . . . *review or check carefully*
    *grow up . . . . *become an adult*

H hand in . . . . *submit an assignment*
    hang up . . . . *(1) conclude a telephone conversation; (2) put clothes on a hanger or a hook*
    have on . . . . *wear*

K keep out (of) . . . . *not enter*
    *keep up (with) . . . . *stay at the same position or level*
    kick out (of) . . . . *force (someone) to leave*

L *look after . . . . *take care of*
    *look into . . . . *investigate*
    *look out (for) . . . . *be careful*
    look over . . . . *review or check carefully*
    look up . . . . *look for information in a reference book*

M make up . . . . *(1) invent; (2) do past due work*

N name after, name for . . . . *give a baby the name of someone else*

P *pass away, *pass on . . . . *die*
    pass out . . . . *distribute*
    *pass out . . . . *lose consciousness*
    pick out . . . . *select*
    pick up . . . . *(1) go to get someone (e.g., in a car); (2) take in one's hand*
    point out . . . . *call attention to*
    put away . . . . *remove to a proper place*
    put back . . . . *return to original place*
    put off . . . . *postpone*
    put on . . . . *put clothes on one's body*
    put out . . . . *extinguish a cigarette, cigar, or fire*
    *put up with . . . . *tolerate*

R *run into, *run across . . . . *meet by chance*
    *run out (of) . . . . *finish a supply of something*

S *show up . . . . *appear, come*
    shut off . . . . *stop a machine, light, faucet*

T *take after . . . . *resemble*
take off . . . . *(1) remove clothing; (2) leave on a trip*
take out . . . . *(1) take someone on a date; (2) remove*
take over . . . . *take control*
take up . . . . *begin a new activity or topic*
tear down . . . . *demolish, reduce to nothing*
tear up . . . . *tear into many little pieces*
think over . . . . *consider carefully*
throw away, throw out . . . . *discard, get rid of*
throw up . . . . *vomit, regurgitate food*
try on . . . . *put on clothing to see if it fits*
turn down . . . . *decrease volume or intensity*
turn in . . . . *(1) submit an assignment; (2) go to bed*
turn off . . . . *stop a machine, light, faucet*
turn on . . . . *start a machine, light, faucet*
turn out . . . . *extinguish a light*
turn up . . . . *increase volume or intensity*

◇ **PRACTICE 1. Phrasal verbs.**

Directions: Supply appropriate prepositions for these two-word and three-word verbs.

1. A: Where did you grow ___up___ ?

   B: In Seattle, Washington.

2. A: I'm trying to find yesterday's newspaper. Have you seen it?

   B: I'm afraid I threw it _____ . I thought you had finished reading it.

3. A: Don't forget to turn the lights _____ before you go to bed.

   B: I won't.

4. A: I have a car, so I can drive us to the festival.

   B: Good.

   A: What time should I pick you _____ ?

   B: Any time after five would be fine.

5. A: We couldn't see the show at the outdoor theater last night.

   B: Why not?

   A: It was called _____ on account of rain.

   B: Did you get a raincheck?

6. A: Thomas looks sad.

   B: I think he misses his girlfriend. Let's try to cheer him _____ .

7. A: I would like to check this book _____ . What should I do?

   B: Take the book to the circulation desk and give the librarian your student I.D.

8. A: What brought _____ your decision to quit your present job?

   B: I was offered a better job.

9. A: How many people showed _____ for the meeting yesterday?

   B: About twenty.

10. A: How was your vacation?

   B: I had a great time.

   A: When did you get _____ home?

   B: A couple of days ago. I had planned to stay a little longer, but I ran _____ _____ money.

◇ PRACTICE 2. Phrasal verbs.

Directions: Supply appropriate prepositions for these two-word and three-word verbs.

1. A: When do we have to turn _____ our assignments?

   B: They're due next Tuesday.

2. A: How does this tape recorder work?

   B: Push this button to turn it _____ , and push that button to shut it _____ .

3. A: May I borrow your dictionary?

   B: Sure. But please be sure to put it _____ on the shelf when you're finished.

4. A: I'm going to be in your neighborhood tomorrow.

   B: Oh? If you have time, why don't you drop _____ to see us?

5. A: Look _____ ! A car is coming!

6. A: I got very irritated at one of my dinner guests last night.

   B: Why?

   A: There was an ashtray on the table, but she put her cigarette _____ on one of my good plates!

7. A: I need to talk to Karen.

   B: Why don't you call her _____ ? She's probably at home now.

8. A: Oh-oh. I made a mistake on the check I just wrote.

   B: Don't try to correct the mistake. Just tear _____ the check and throw it _____ .

9. A: Are you here to apply for a job?

   B: Yes.

   A: Here is an application form. Fill it _____ and then give it _____ to me when you are finished.

10. A: Look. There's Mike.

    B: Where?

    A: At the other end of the block, walking toward the administration building. If we run, we can catch _____ with him.

11. A: Is your roommate here?

    B: Yes. She decided to come to the party after all. Have you ever met her?

    A: No, but I'd like to.

    B: She's the one standing over there by the far window. She has a blue dress _____ . Come on. I'll introduce you.

12. A: Do you have a date for Saturday night?

    B: Yes. Jim Brock asked me _____ . We're going bowling.

◇ **PRACTICE 3. Phrasal verbs.**

Directions: Supply appropriate prepositions for these two-word and three-word verbs.

1. A: I think we should increase the membership dues from one dollar to two.

    B: That might solve some of our financial problems. Why don't you bring that _____ at the next meeting?

2. A: Did you hand _____ your composition?

    B: No. I didn't like it, so I decided to do it _____ .

3. A: What time did you get _____ this morning?

    B: I slept late. I didn't drag myself out of bed until after nine.

4. A: What's the baby's name?

    B: Helen. She was named _____ her paternal grandmother.

5. A: I need to get more exercise.

    B: Why don't you take _____ tennis?

6. A: You can't go in there.

    B: Why not?

    A: Look at that sign. It says, "Keep _____ . No trespassing."

7. A: I can't reach Fred. There's a busy signal.

    B: Then hang _____ and try again later.

8. A: The radio is too loud. Would you mind if I turned it _____ a little?

    B: No.

9. A: I can't hear the radio. Could you turn it _____ a little?

    B: Sure.

10. A: What are you doing Saturday night, Bob?

    B: I'm taking Virginia _____ for dinner and a show.

◇ **PRACTICE 4. Phrasal verbs.**

Directions: Supply appropriate prepositions for these two-word and three-word verbs.

1. A: Omar, would you please pass these papers _____ to the rest of the class?

   B: I'd be happy to.

2. A: When are we expected to be at the hotel?

   B: According to our reservation, we are supposed to check _____ the hotel before

   6 P.M. Monday and check _____ before noon Tuesday.

3. A: How do you get _____ with your roommate?

   B: Fine. He's a nice guy.

4. A: Thanks for the ride. I appreciate it.

   B: Where should I drop you _____ ?

   A: The next corner would be fine.

5. A: I'm going to be out of town for a couple of days. Would you mind looking

   _____ my cat?

   B: Not at all. I'd be happy to. Just tell me what I'm supposed to do.

6. A: I think I'm going to turn _____ now. Good night.

   B: 'Night. See you in the morning. Sleep well.

7. A: Don't you think it's hot in here?

   B: Not especially. If you're hot, why don't you take your sweater _____ ?

8: A: How do you spell "occasionally"?

   B: I'm not sure. You'd better look it _____ in your dictionary.

9. A: How much lettuce should we get?

   B: I think we could use two heads. Pick _____ two that feel fresh and firm.

10. A: Why are you sniffling?

    B: I had a cold last week, and I can't seem to get _____ it.

◇ **PRACTICE 5. Phrasal verbs.**

Directions: Supply appropriate prepositions for these two-word and three-word verbs.

1. A: Are you ready to leave?

   B: Almost. I'll be ready to go just as soon as I get _____ putting the clean dishes

   away.

2. A: I'm going crazy! I've been trying to solve this math problem for the last hour, and I still

   can't get it.

   B: Why don't you give _____ for a while? Take a break and then go back to it.

3. A: I hear you had a frightening experience yesterday. What happened?

   B: Ed suddenly got dizzy and then passed _____ . I tried to revive him, but he was out cold. Luckily there was a doctor in the building.

4. A: What happened when the pilot of the plane passed out during the flight?

   B: The co-pilot took _____ .

5. A: Cindy is only three. She likes to play with the older kids, but when they're running and playing, she can't keep _____ with them.

   B: Does she mind?

   A: She doesn't seem to.

6. A: I made a mistake in my composition. What should I do?

   B: Since it's an in-class composition, just cross it _____ .

7. A: I need my dictionary, but I lent it to Jose.

   B: Why don't you get it _____ from him?

8. A: I wish the teacher wouldn't call _____ me in class.

   B: Why not?

   A: I get nervous.

   B: Why?

   A: I don't know.

9. I took a plane from Atlanta to Miami. I got _____ the plane in Atlanta. I got _____ the plane in Miami.

10. It was a snowy winter day, but I still had to drive to work. First I got _____ the car to start the engine. Then I got _____ of the car to scrape the snow and ice from the windows.

11. Last year I took a train trip. I got _____ the train in Chicago. I got _____ the train in Des Moines.

12. Phyllis takes the bus to work. She gets _____ the bus at Lindbergh Boulevard and gets _____ the bus about two blocks from her office on Tower Street.

◇ **PRACTICE 6. Phrasal verbs.**
   Directions: Supply appropriate prepositions for these two-word and three-word verbs.

   1. A: Why don't we try to call _____ the O'Briens sometime this weekend? We haven't seen them for a long time.

      B: Good idea. I'd like to see them again.

2. A: Did you go _____ your paper carefully before you handed it _____ ?

   B: Yes. I looked it _____ carefully.

3. A: Do you believe his story about being late because he had a flat tire?

   B: No. I think he made it _____ .

4. A: Could you pick _____ a newspaper on your way home from work tonight?

   B: Sure.

5. A: Did you hear the bad news?

   B: About what?

   A: Gary's grandmother passed _____ . Gary went home to be with his family and attend the funeral.

6. A: I like your new shoes.

   B: Thanks. I had to try _____ almost a dozen pairs before I decided to get these.

7. A: Have you decided to accept that new job?

   B: Not yet. I'm still thinking it _____ .

8. A: I'm tired. I wish I could get _____ of going to the meeting tonight.

   B: Do you have to go?

9. A: Why hasn't Mary been in class for the last two weeks?

   B: She dropped _____ _____ school.

10. A: What time does your plane take _____ ?

   B: 10:40.

   A: How long does the flight take?

   B: I think we get _____ around 12:30.

11. A: Do you like living in the dorm?

   B: It's okay. I've learned to put _____ with all the noise.

12. A: What brought _____ your decision to quit your job?

   B: I couldn't get _____ _____ my boss.

◇ **PRACTICE 7. Phrasal verbs.**

Directions: Supply appropriate prepositions for each of these two-word verbs.

1. A: Guess who I ran _____ today as I was walking across campus.

   B: Who?

   A: Ann Keefe.

   B: You're kidding!

2. A: There will be a test on Chapters Eight and Nine next Friday.

   B: *(Groan.)* Couldn't you put it _____ until Monday?

3. A: You'd better put _____ your coat before you leave. It's chilly out.

   B: What's the temperature?

4. A: I smell something burning in the kitchen. Can I call you _____ in a minute?

   B: Sure. I hope your dinner hasn't burned.

   A: So do I! Bye.

   B: Good-bye.

5. A: I think that if I learn enough vocabulary I won't have any trouble using English.

   B: That's not necessarily so. I'd like to point _____ that language consists of much
   more than just vocabulary.

6. A: One billion seconds ago, World War II was being fought. One billion minutes ago, Jesus
   Christ was living. One billion hours ago, the human race had not yet discovered
   agriculture.

   B: How did you figure that _____?

   A: I didn't. I came _____ that information while I was reading the newspaper.

7. A: Your children certainly love the outdoors.

   B: Yes, they do. We brought them _____ to appreciate nature.

8. A: What forms do I have to fill out to change my tourist visa to a student visa?

   B: I don't know, but I'll look _____ it first thing tomorrow and try to find _____ .
   I'll let you know.

9. A: How long were you in the hospital?

   B: About a week. But I've missed almost two weeks of classes.

   A: It's going to be hard for you to make _____ all the work you've missed, isn't it?

   B: Very.

10. A: Would you mind turning _____ the light?

    B: Not at all.

◇ **PRACTICE 8. Phrasal verbs.**

Directions: Supply appropriate prepositions for these two-word verbs.

1. A: Who do you take _____ the most, your father or your mother?

   B: My mother, I think. I can see many similarities between the two of us.

2. A: Hey, cut it _____, you guys! I'm trying to sleep.

   B: What's the matter? Are we making too much noise?

3. A: Could I help you clean _____?

   B: Sure. Would you mind taking _____ the garbage?

4. A: Miss Ward, what seems to be the problem?

   B: Well, Doctor, for the last two days I haven't been able to keep any food down. Every time I try to eat something, I throw _____ soon afterward.

5. A: Where's my jacket?

   B: I hung it _____ the closet.

6. A: Why are you going to see Professor Kelly?

   B: He called me _____ to talk about my research project.

7. A: Is that man's story true?

   B: Yes. A newspaper reporter checked _____ his story and found that it was true.

8. A: The city government is planning to redevelop a large section of the inner city.

   B: What's going to happen to the buildings that are there now?

   A: They are going to be torn _____.

9. A: Some people tried to crash our party last night.

   B: What did you do?

   A: We kicked them _____.

10. The test is about to begin. Please put _____ all of your books and notebooks.

Index

Answer Key

To the student: To make it easy to correct your own answers, remove this answer key along the perforations and make a separate answer key booklet for yourself.

Chapter 12: NOUN CLAUSES

◇ **PRACTICE 1, p. 116.**
1. Q (?)
2. N.Cl. (.)
3. Q (?)
4. N.Cl. (.)
5. Q (?)
6. N.Cl. (.)
7. N.Cl. (.)
8. Q (?)
9. Q (?)
10. N.Cl. (?) [Note: *who she is* is a noun clause; the whole sentence is a question.]
11. Q (?)
12. N.Cl. (.)

◇ **PRACTICE 2, p. 116.**
1. Where (?)
2. I don't know (.)
3. I don't know (.)
4. What (?)
5. How (?)
6. I don't know (.)
7. Where (?)
8. I don't know (.)
9. I don't know (.)
10. Why (?)
11. I don't know (.)
12. Who (?)
13. When (?)
14. I don't know (.)
15. Who (?)
16. I don't know (.)

◇ **PRACTICE 3, p. 117.**
1. Who is that man? . . . who that man is.
2. Where does George live? . . . where George lives.
3. What did Ann buy? . . . what Ann bought.
4. How far is it to Denver from here? . . . how far it is to Denver from here.
5. Why was Jack late to class? . . . why Jack was late to class.
6. Whose pen is that? . . . whose pen that is.

7. Who(m) did Alex see at the meeting? . . . who(m) Alex saw at the meeting.
8. Who saw Ms. Frost at the meeting? . . . who saw Ms. Frost at the meeting.
9. Which book does Alice like best? . . . which book Alice likes best.
10. When/What time is the plane supposed to land? . . . when/what time the plane is supposed to land.

◇ **PRACTICE 4, p. 118.**
1. A: *Where* does Fred live?
   B: (. . .) wants to know where Fred lives.
2. A: *What* time is it?
   B: (. . .) wants to know what time it is.
3. A: *What* does Tom want for his birthday?
   B: (. . .) wants to know what Tom wants for his birthday.
   C: He wants a watch.
4. A: *How* does Jane get to school?
   B: (. . .) wants to know how Jane gets to school.
   C: By bus.
5. A: *When* does vacation start?
   B: . . . wants to know when vacation starts.
   C: On June 3rd [= third].
6. A: *Why* did Sue leave class early?
   B: . . . wants to know why Sue left class early.
   C: Because she didn't feel well.
7. A: *How* long is the movie going to last?
   B: . . . wants to know how long the movie is going to last.
   C: Two hours and ten minutes
8. A: *Who(m)* did Mary call?
   B: . . . wants to know who(m) Mary called.
   C: Jim
9. A: *Who* called Jim?
   B: . . . wants to know who called Jim.
   C: Mary.
10. A: *What* did Alice talk to the teacher about?
    B: . . . wants to know what Alice talked to the teacher about.
    C: The test.
11. A: *Who(m)* did Alice talk to about the test?
    (Formal: To whom did Alice talk about the test?)
    B: (. . .) wants to know who(m) Alice talked to about the test. *(Formal:* (. . .) wants to know to whom Alice talked about the test.)
    C: The teacher.

1

12. A: *Who* talked to the teacher about the test?
    B: (. . .) wants to know who talked to the teacher about the test.
    C: Alice.
13. A: *When/At what time* will Sue's plane arrive?
    B: (. . .) wants to know when/at what time Sue's plane will arrive.
    C: At 8:05.
14. A: *How many* students will be absent from class tomorrow?
    B: (. . .) wants to know how many students will be absent from class tomorrow.
    C: Two.
15. A: *How many* lakes are there in Minnesota?
    B: (. . .) wants to know how many lakes there are in Minnesota.
    C: 10,000.
16. A: *How far/How many miles* is it to Springfield from here?
    B: (. . .) wants to know how far/how many miles it is to Springfield from here.
    C: 25.
17. A: *What* did Jane do last night?
    B: (. . .) wants to know what Jane did last night.
    C: Studied.
18. A: *Which* book are we supposed to buy?
    B: (. . .) wants to know which book we're supposed to buy.
    C: This book.
19. A: *What kind of* ice cream does Ann like the best?
    B: (. . .) wants to know what kind of ice cream Ann likes the best.
    C: Chocolate.
20. A: *What* color is a robin's egg?
    B: (. . .) wants to know what color a robin's egg is.
    C: Turquoise blue. [TURQUOISE is pronounced /tərkwɔiz/]
21. A: *Who* is that woman?
    B: (. . .) wants to know who that woman is.
    C: Mrs. Anderson.
22. A: *Who* is talking on the telephone?
    B: (. . .) wants to know who is talking on the telephone.
    C: Mr. Anderson.
23. A: *Whose* notebook is that?
    B: (. . .) wants to know whose notebook that is.
    C: Sam's.
24. A: *Whose* car was stolen?
    B: (. . .) wants to know whose car was stolen.
    C: Jessica's.

◇ **PRACTICE 5, p. 119.**
1. A: he's looking for
   B: are you looking for
2. A: did he decide
   B: he decided
3. A: is this
   B: it is
4. A: did he buy
   B: he bought
5. A: John's tutor is
   B: is John's tutor
6. A: didn't you study
   B: I didn't study

◇ **PRACTICE 6, p. 120.**
1. if/whether it will rain
2. when it will rain
3. if/whether Sam is
4. where Sam is
5. if/whether Jane called
6. what time she called
7. why the earth is called
8. how far it is
9. if/whether Susan has ever been
10. if/whether she speaks
11. who Ann played
12. who won
13. if/whether Ann won
14. if/whether all creatures, including fish and insects, feel
15. if/whether birds can communicate
16. how birds communicate
17. where the nearest post office is
18. if/whether there is a post office

◇ **PRACTICE 7, p. 122.**
1. where to buy
2. whether to stay . . . go
3. how to fix
4. whether (or not) to look
5. where to get
6. whether (or not) to go
7. what time to pick
8. who to talk
9. whether to take . . . to do
10. how to solve
11. where to tell
12. how long to cook
13. what to wear
14. how much coffee to make
15. which essay to use
16. whether to take . . . travel . . . (to) keep . . . save

◇ **PRACTICE 8, p. 123.**
1. It is surprising that no one stopped to help Sam when he had car trouble.
   That no one stopped to help Sam when he had car trouble is surprising.
2. It is unfortunate that people in modern cities are distrustful of each other.
   That people in modern cities are distrustful of each other is unfortunate.
3. It is still true that people in my village always help each other.
   That people in my village always help each other is still true.
4. It is undeniably true that people need each other and need to help each other.
   That people need each other and need to help each other is undeniably true.
5. It seems obvious to me that people have a moral duty to help others in need.
   That people have a moral duty to help others in need seems obvious to me.
6. It is a pity that people today are afraid to help strangers.
   That people today are afraid to help strangers is a pity.

7. It seems strange to me that people in cities live in densely populated areas but don't know their neighbors.

That people in cities live in densely populated areas but don't know their neighbors seems strange to me.

◇ **PRACTICE 9, p. 123.**

1. *Regardless of* **the fact that** *I studied for three months for the examination,* I barely passed.
2. There's nothing we can do *about* **the fact that** *Jim lost our tickets to the concert.*
3. **The fact that** *we are going to miss one of the best concerts of the year because of Jim's carelessness* makes me a little angry.
4. In *view of* **the fact that** *we can't go to the concert,* let's plan to go to a movie.
5. *Except for* **the fact that** *I couldn't speak a word of Italian and understood very little,* I had a wonderful time visiting my Italian cousins in Rome.
6. When I first visited Florida, I was surprised *by* **the fact that** *many people living in Miami speak only Spanish.*
7. **The fact that** *Bobby broke my grandmother's antique flower vase* isn't important.
8. **The fact that** *he lied about it* is what bothers me.
9. At first, some of us objected *to* **the fact that** *Prof. Brown, who had almost no teaching experience, was hired to teach the advanced physics course,* but she has proven herself to be one of the best.
10. I am impressed *by* **the fact that** *that automobile has the best safety record of any car manufactured this year* and would definitely recommend that you buy that make.

◇ **PRACTICE 10, p. 124.**

1. The athlete said, "**W**here is my uniform?"
2. "I can't remember," Margaret said, "where I put my purse."
3. Sandy asked her sister, "**H**ow can I help you get through this difficulty?"
4. "I'll answers your question later," he whispered. "**I**'m trying to hear what the speaker is saying."
5. As the students entered the room, the teacher said, "**P**lease take your seats quickly."
6. "Why did I ever take this job?" Barry wondered aloud.
7. After crashing into me and knocking all of my packages to the ground, the man stopped abruptly, turned to me, and said softly, "Excuse me."
8. "Do we want four more years of corruption and debt?" the candidate shouted into the microphone. "No!" the crowd screamed.
9. The woman behind the fast-food counter shouted, "**W**ho's next?"
   "I am," three people replied at the same time.
   "Which one of you is really next?" she asked impatiently.
   "I was here first," said a young woman elbowing her way up to the counter. "I want a hamburger."
   "You were not!" hollered an older man standing next to her. "I was here before you were. **G**ive me a chicken sandwich and a cup of coffee."
   "Wait a minute! I was in line first," said a young man. "**G**ive me a cheeseburger and a chocolate shake."

The woman behind the restaurant counter spotted a little boy politely waiting his turn. **S**he turned to him and said, "**H**i, Sonny. **W**hat can I get for you?"

◇ **PRACTICE 11, p. 126.**

1. was
2. needed
3. was having
4. had finished
5. had finished
6. would arrive
7. was going to be/would be
8. could solve
9. might come
10. might come
11. had to leave
12. had to leave
13. should go
14. ought to go
15. to stay
16. not to move
17. was
18. had arrived

◇ **PRACTICE 12, p. 126.**

1. if/whether she was planning
2. what time the movie begins
3. if/whether we could still get
4. how he can help
5. if/whether he could help
6. when the final decision would be made
7. where she had been
8. what Kim's native language is
9. what the problem was
10. if/whether I was doing
11. when this terrible drought is going
12. what time he had
13. who(m) she should give the message to
14. (that) we would be leaving
15. why we hadn't called

◇ **PRACTICE 13, p. 127.**

1. knew . . . had known . . . wanted
2. still smoked . . . had tried . . . didn't seem
3. what the capital of Australia was/is . . . wasn't . . . thought it was
4. would be . . . would . . . left
5. was pouring . . . had better take . . . would stop . . . didn't need
6. was going . . . was . . . asked/invited . . . would like . . . had . . . had . . . was . . . could . . . were
7. The passenger sitting next to me on the plane *asked* me where I *was* from. I *told* her I *was* from Chicago. She *said* that she *was* from Mapleton, a small town in northern Michigan. She wondered if I *had heard* of it, and I told her that I *had.* [British: *had done*] I went on to say that I thought Michigan *was* a beautiful state and explained that I had *been* there on vacation many times. She *asked* me if I *had been* in Michigan on vacation this year. I replied that I *hadn't (been)* and *told* her that I *had gone* far away, to India. Then she asked me if it *was* a long drive . . . .

PRACTICE 14, p. 129.

1. organize
2. be divided
3. call
4. be told
5. open
6. take
7. be
8. be mailed
9. obey
10. be given

PRACTICE 15, p. 130.

1. whenever
2. wherever
3. whatever
4. whichever
5. whatever
6. who(m)ever
7. whichever
8. Whoever
9. whatever
10. wherever

PRACTICE 16. Test A, p. 131.

1. B
2. C
3. B
4. D
5. A
6. A
7. D
8. D
9. A
10. B
11. B
12. A
13. D
14. D
15. D
16. B
17. C
18. C
19. A
20. B

PRACTICE 17. Test B, p. 133.

1. A
2. C
3. D
4. D
5. C
6. B
7. B
8. C
9. C
10. A
11. D
12. D
13. B
14. D
15. A
16. D
17. B
18. C
19. A
20. C

Chapter 13: ADJECTIVE CLAUSES

PRACTICE 1, p. 135.

1. a. that are marked with a small red dot
   b. which are marked with a small red dot
2. a. who sits at the first desk on the right
   b. that sits at the first desk on the right
3. a. that I bought
   b. which I bought
   c. I bought
4. a. that I met at the meeting
   b. who(m) I met at the meeting
   c. I met at the meeting
5. a. we listened to last night
   b. that we listened to last night
   c. which we listened to last night
   d. to which we listened last night
6. a. I told you about
   b. who(m) I told you about
   c. that I told you about
   d. about whom I told you

7. whose parents you just met
8. who played at the concert last night
9. a waiter has to serve
10. Bob recommended
11. whose book on time and space has been translated into dozens of languages
12. who lives next door to us

PRACTICE 2, p. 136.

1. who(m)/that/Ø
2. who/that
3. which/that/Ø
4. which
5. who(m)/that/Ø
6. who/that
7. whose
8. whom
9. which/that

PRACTICE 3, p. 137.

1. which/that
2. who/that
3. which/that
4. which/that
5. who/that
6. which/that/Ø
7. who(m)/that/Ø
8. which/that/Ø
9. which
10. which/that/Ø
11. whom
12. who(m)/that/Ø

PRACTICE 4, p. 138.

1. Louis knows the woman *who/that is meeting us at the airport.*
2. The chair *which/that/Ø Sally inherited from her grandmother* is an antique.
3. The bench *which/that/Ø I sat on* was wet. OR: The bench *on which I sat* was wet.
4. The man *who(m)/that/Ø I hired to paint my house* finished the job in four days.
5. I miss seeing the old woman *who/that used to sell flowers on that street corner.*
6. The architect *who(m)/that/Ø Mario works with* is brilliant. OR: The architect *with whom Mario works* is brilliant.
7. Mary tutors students *who/that need extra help in geometry.*
8. I took a picture of the rainbow *which/that appeared in the sky after the shower.*

PRACTICE 5, p. 138.

1. Do you know the man *whose car is parked over there?*
2. I know a woman *whose name is May Day.*
3. The people *whose home we visited* were very hospitable.
4. The school principal walked down the hallway to find the boy *whose parents had been injured in an automobile accident.*
5. Mrs. Lake is the teacher *whose class I enjoy the most.*
6. Any company *whose employees are in constant fear of losing their jobs* is stifling the creativity of its workforce.

◇ PRACTICE 6, p. 139.

1. That is the room where we have class.
2. That is the restaurant where we ate dinner.
3. That is the building where Anna works.
4. That is the year when I was born.
5. That is the cafeteria where you eat lunch.
6. That is the month when the monsoons arrive.
7. That is the street where Alex lives.
8. That is the island where you spent your vacation.
9. That is the lake where you went swimming.
10. That is the town where you grew up.
11. That is the day when the space flight to Mars is scheduled to leave.
12. That is the country where the earthquake occurred.
13. That is the room where the examination will be given.
14. That is the city where you lived until you were ten years old.
15. That is the time when you felt the happiest.

◇ PRACTICE 7, p. 139.

1. A, D	5. D	9. B, C, D
2. B, C, D	6. B, C	10. B
3. C, D	7. A	11. A
4. B	8. C, D	12. A

◇ PRACTICE 8, p. 140.

1. speak	8. have
2. speaks	9. are
3. are . . . don't	10. state . . . wish
4. offers are	
5. measures . . . walks	
6. suffer	
7. have	

◇ PRACTICE 9, p. 140.

1. NO
2. YES . . . I made an appointment with Dr. Raven, who is considered an expert on eye disorders.
3. NO
4. NO
5. YES . . . Bogota, which is the capital of Colombia, is a cosmopolitan city.
6. YES . . . They climbed Mount Rainier, which is in the state of Washington, twice last year.
7. YES . . . Emeralds, which are valuable gemstones, are mined in Colombia.
8. YES . . . The company offered the position to John, whose department performed best this year.
9. YES . . . On our trip to Africa we visited Nairobi, which is near several fascinating game reserves, and then traveled to Egypt to see the pyramids.
10. NO
11. NO
12. YES . . . Larry was very close to his only brother, who was a famous social historian.
13. NO
14. NO
15. YES . . . A typhoon, which is a violent tropical storm, can cause great destruction.
16. NO

◇ PRACTICE 10, p. 141.

1. A	6. B	11. A, D
2. A, D	7. A	12. A
3. C	8. C	13. C, D, E
4. A	9. A, D	
5. A, B, D, E	10. A	

◇ PRACTICE 11, p. 142.

1. a	5. b
2. b	6. a
3. a	7. b
4. b	8. a

◇ PRACTICE 12, p. 143.

1. YES . . . Thirty people, two of whom were members of the crew, were killed in the ferry accident.
2. NO
3. YES . . . Over 500 students took the entrance examination, the results of which will be posted in the administration building at the end of the month.
4. NO
5. NO
6. YES . . . The new supervisor was not happy with his work crew, none of whom seemed interested in doing quality work.
7. YES . . . My oldest brother, in whose house I lived for six months when I was ten, has been a father to me in many ways.
8. YES . . . Tom is always interrupting me, which makes me mad.
9. YES . . . To express the uselessness of worrying, Mark Twain once said, "I've had a lot of problems in my life, most of which never happened."

◇ PRACTICE 13, p. 143.

1. . . . offers, **neither of which** I accepted.
2. . . . three brothers, **two of whom** are professional athletes.
3. . . . business ventures, **only one of which** is profitable.
4. . . . fifty states, **the majority of which** are located . . . .
5. The two women, **both of whom** are changing careers, have already dissolved . . . .
6. . . . success, **much of which** has been due to hard work, but **some of which** has been due to good luck.

◇ PRACTICE 14, p. 143.

1. Only a few of the movies *shown at the Gray Theater* are suitable for children.
2. We visited Madrid, *the capital of Spain.*
3. The couple *living in the house next door* are both college professors.
4. Astronomy, *the study of planets and stars,* is one of the world's oldest sciences.
5. Only a small fraction of the eggs *laid by a fish* actually hatch and survive to adulthood.
6. Jasmine, *a viny plant with fragrant flowers,* grows only in warm places.
7. Arizona, *once thought to be a useless desert,* is today a rapidly growing industrial and agricultural state.
8. Simon Bolivar, *a great South American general,* led the fight for independence early in the 19th century.

9. In hot weather, many people enjoy lemonade, *a drink made from lemon juice, water, and sugar.*
10. I was awakened by the sound of laughter *coming from the room next to mine at the motel.*
11. Few tourists ever see a jaguar, *a spotted cat native to tropical America.*

◇ PRACTICE 15, p. 144.

1. A national holiday has been established in memory of Martin Luther King, Jr.**,** the leader of the civil rights movement in the United States in the 1950s and 1960s.
2. Neil Armstrong**,** the first person to set foot on the moon**,** reported that the surface was fine and powdery.
3. Mark Twain is an author known far and wide as one of the greatest American humorists. *(no commas)*
4. Susan B. Anthony**,** one of the first leaders of the campaign for women's rights**,** worked tirelessly during her lifetime to gain the right to vote for women.

◇ PRACTICE 16, p. 144.

1. Louisville, the largest city in Kentucky, was founded in 1778.
2. John Quincy Adams, the sixth president of the United States, was born on July 11, 1767.
3. Two languages, Finnish and Swedish, are used in Helsinki, the capital of Finland.
4. The Washington National Monument, a towering obelisk made of white marble, is a famous landmark in the nation's capital.
5. Honolulu, best known to the traveler for Waikiki Beach, has consistently pleasant weather.
6. Libya, a country in North Africa, is a leading producer of oil.

◇ PRACTICE 17, p. 145.

1. None of the pedestrians *walking up and down the busy street* stopped to help or even inquire about the elderly man *slumped in the doorway of an apparently unoccupied building.*
2. Food *passing from the mouth to the stomach* goes through a tube *called the esophagus.*
3. Animals *born in a zoo* generally adjust to captivity better than those *captured in the wild.*
4. The children attended a special movie program *consisting of cartoons featuring Donald Duck and Mickey Mouse.*
5. One of the most important foodstuffs in the world is flour, *a fine powder made by grinding wheat or other grains.*
6. Nero, *Emperor of Rome from A.D. 54 to 68,* is believed to have murdered both his mother and his wife.
7. The conclusion *presented in that book* states that most of the automobiles *produced by American industry in the 1960s and '70s* had some defect.
8. Pictures *showing the brutality of war* entered the living rooms of millions of TV watchers on the nightly news.
9. The Indians *living in Peru before the discovery of the New World by Europeans* belonged to the Incan culture.

10. My uncle Elias, *a restaurant owner,* often buys fish and shellfish from boats *docked at the local pier.* Customers come from miles around to dine on a seafood feast *considered to be the best in all of the northeastern United States.*
11. Hundreds of volunteers went to a northern village yesterday to reinforce firefighters *trying to save a settlement threatened by a forest fire.* The fire started when a cigarette ignited oil *leaking from a machine used to cut timber.*
12. Researchers have developed a way to mark genes so that they glow in the dark, *a technique that scientists can use to follow specific genetic activity of cells within plants and animals.* This development, *announced by the National Science Foundation, the sponsor of the research,* should prove useful to scientists *studying the basic functions of organisms.*

◇ PRACTICE 18, p. 146.

1. . . . a lot of people **waiting** in a long line . . .
2. Students who **live** on campus . . . OR: Students (omit *who*) **living** on campus . . . .
3. . . . the librarian **who/that** sits at . . . OR: the librarian **sitting** at . . . .
4. . . . sister is Anna, **who** is 21 years old. OR: sister, Anna, is 21 years old.
5. . . . in Sapporo, **which** is a city . . . OR: . . . in Sapporo, (omit *that is*) a city . . . .
6. Patrick, **who** is my oldest brother, is married and . . . OR: Patrick, my oldest brother, **is** married and . . . .
7. The person **who sits/sitting** next to me is someone **who(m)/that/Ø** I've never met (omit *him*).
8. . . . a small city (omit *is*) located . . . OR: . . . a small city **which/that** is located . . . .
9. Last Saturday, I attended a party **given** by one of my friends. My friend, **whose** apartment is in another town, was very glad that I could come.
10. Dr. Darnell was the only person **who(m)/that/Ø** I wanted to see.
11. There are eighty **students from** all over the **world studying** English at this school. OR: . . . students from all over the world **who study** . . . *(no commas)*
12. The people **who(m)/that/Ø** we met on our trip last May are going to visit us in October.
13. Dianne Jones, **who used to teach Spanish**, has organized a tour of . . . .
14. . . . since I came **here, some of whom** are from my country. OR: . . . **here. Some of them** . . . .
15. People **who** *(also possible but not preferred:* that) can speak English can be . . . .

◇ PRACTICE 19. Test A, p. 147.

1. D	11. C
2. A	12. B
3. B	13. C
4. D	14. D
5. B	15. D
6. A	16. B
7. C	17. D
8. D	18. B
9. C	19. A
10. A	20. C

1. C	11. D
2. B	12. B
3. A	13. C
4. A	14. B
5. C	15. A
6. B	16. C
7. D	17. D
8. D	18. C
9. B	19. A
10. C	20. B

Chapter 14: GERUNDS AND INFINITIVES, PART 1

◇ **PRACTICE 1, p. 151.**
1. of asking
2. to seeing
3. of washing
4. for breaking
5. from opening
6. of talking
7. like having
8. to killing
9. about finishing
10. for locking . . . (for) making
11. of practicing

◇ **PRACTICE 2, p. 152.**

Expected completions:
1. I thanked my classmate for helping me with my homework.
2. The treasurer is responsible for balancing the checkbook.
3. The students complained about having too many tests.
4. I apologized for stepping on my friend's toe.
5. A bodybuilder is capable of lifting heavy weights.
6. A teacher is used to answering students' questions.
7. The rainy weather prevented us from going on a picnic.
8. All of the children participated in making decorations for their classroom.
9. Unauthorized persons are prohibited from entering a military base.
10. The little girl was excited about getting a new doll for her birthday.
11. I thanked the flight attendant for getting me a pillow.
12. The employees objected to being forced to work overtime.

◇ **PRACTICE 3, p. 152.**

Sample responses:
1. I *enjoy taking* long walks in the evening.
2. Pierre *avoids eating* spicy food.
3. I often *go jogging* in the morning.
4. When I *finished doing* the housework, I took a break.

5. Yoko *suggested changing* the time of our lunch date from 11:30 to noon.
6. I'm *considering going swimming* at the beach after work today.
7. The little girl *stopped crying* when I handed her her doll.
8. Mary and Bob *discussed going shopping* for new furniture sometime this week.
9. Tarik *mentioned having to go* to the doctor's office today.
10. Tom *delayed putting* his tools away until he had completely finished the job.
11. Would you *mind taking* this letter with you when you go to the post office?
12. The children *kept asking* for ice cream.
13. I *quit worrying about* my grade in my economics class after I passed the final exam.
14. Sam *postponed taking* his two-week vacation until August.

◇ **PRACTICE 4, p. 153.**
1. We spent all yesterday afternoon playing soccer.
2. All of us had a really good time playing soccer in the park yesterday.
3. Omar had trouble finding my house last night.
4. My mother caught some neighborhood kids trying to steal my bicycle yesterday.
5. When the boss walked into the office, all of the employees were standing at the window watching the parade on the street below. OR: All of the employees were standing at the window watching the parade on the street below when the boss walked into the office.
6. My father always said, "Don't waste your time reading novels when you could be learning something worthwhile from other kinds of books."
7. When Mrs. Smith checked on the children last night, she found them playing a game instead of sleeping.
8. When I opened the door, I found Susan lying on her bed crying. OR: I found Susan lying on her bed crying when I opened the door.

◇ **PRACTICE 5, p. 153.**

1. B	11. B
2. B	12. A
3. A	13. A
4. A	14. A
5. B	15. B
6. B	16. B
7. A	17. B
8. B	18. B
9. B	19. A
10. A	20. A

◇ **PRACTICE 6, p. 154.**
1. asked Jim to give
2. were warned not to park
3. reminded him to brush

4. are required to wear
5. advised me to consult
6. was ordered to leave
7. were expected to complete
8. reminded my husband to buy
9. advised me to get
10. were warned not to be
11. is permitted to use
12. asked her father to buy
13. encouraged our grandfather to write
14. was ordered not to shout

◇ PRACTICE 7, p. 155.

1. During the water shortage, the public *was asked to curtail* its use of water as much as possible.
2. Laura *reminded her roommate not to forget* to set her alarm clock for 6:00.
3. Mrs. Jones *allowed each of the children to have* one piece of candy.
4. The doctor *advised my father to limit* his sugar consumption.
5. My parents often *encouraged me to be* independent.
6. The children *were warned not to swim* in the lake without an adult present.
7. The police officer *ordered the reckless driver to pull over.*
8. Rose *invited Jerry to come* to her house Sunday night to meet her parents.

◇ PRACTICE 8, p. 156.

1. B	14. A, B
2. A, B	15. B
3. A, B	16. A
4. A, B	17. B
5. A, B	18. A
6. B	19. B
7. A, B	20. A
8. B	21. A
9. A, B	22. B
10. A, B	23. A
11. A	24. B
12. B	25. A, B
13. A, B	26. B

◇ PRACTICE 9, p. 157.

(The answers are included in the Practice.)

◇ PRACTICE 10, p. 158.

1. to refund	14. singing
2. to be	15. avoiding
3. to buy	16. to count
4. throwing	17. painting
5. to get	18. to get
6. to wear	19. paying
7. to visit	20. to keep
8. to be	21. taking
9. thinking	22. to know
10. to attend	23. moving
11. to leave	24. to watch
12. to cut	25. to keep
13. to ignore	

◇ PRACTICE 11, p. 160.

1. to operate	14. to see
2. to shoot	15. to go
3. having	16. taking
4. to go	17. to speak
5. getting	18. receiving
6. to attend	19. to meet
7. to come	20. getting
8. to turn	21. staying
9. to tell	22. to apologize
10. practicing	23. to obey
11. to clean	24. seeing
12. reading	25. to take
13. sending	

◇ PRACTICE 12, p. 161.

1. A	6. A	11. B
2. B	7. B	12. B
3. A	8. B	13. A
4. A	9. A	14. B
5. B	10. A	15. B

◇ PRACTICE 13, p. 162.

1. playing
2. (someone) to save
3. telling
4. to get
5. someone to take
6. staying
7. (someone) not to buy
8. giving
9. going
10. travel(l)ing
11. taking
12. (someone) to go swimming
13. being
14. hearing
15. to tell
16. being
17. eating
18. to know
19. to get
20. saying
21. seeing
22. (someone) to give
23. to hire someone to work
24. to tell someone to be/telling someone to be [with different meanings]
25. (someone) to practice speaking
26. (someone) to keep trying to call

◇ PRACTICE 14, p. 163.

1. It is cruel to tease animals.
2. Finding their house wasn't difficult.
3. It is important to vote in every election.
4. Meeting the king and queen was exciting.
5. It would be interesting to hear the other side of the story.
6. Seeing Joan awake early in the morning is unusual.
7. If you know how, floating in the water for a long time is easy.

8. It takes time and patience to master a second language.
9. It will take us ten hours to drive to Atlanta.
10. Diving into the sea from a high cliff takes courage.

Chapter 15: GERUNDS AND INFINITIVES, PART 2

◇ **PRACTICE 1, p. 164.**

1. Ø
2. in order
3. in order
4. in order
5. Ø
6. Ø
7. in order
8. in order
9. Ø
10. in order
11. in order
12. Ø . . . Ø

◇ **PRACTICE 2, p. 165.**

Possible completions:
1. to get
2. to find out
3. to be
4. to fight
5. to go
6. to stay . . . (to) read
7. to help
8. to learn
9. to slip
10. to walk
11. to walk
12. to be
13. to see
14. to hear

◇ **PRACTICE 3, p. 165.**

1. very
2. too
3. too
4. very
5. too
6. too
7. very
8. too
9. very
10. very
11. very . . . too
12. too
13. very
14. too
15. too

◇ **PRACTICE 4, p. 166.**

1. I didn't have enough time to finish my work yesterday.
2. Linda isn't well enough to go back to work.
3. Scissors are too sharp for very young children to use.
4. The streets in the old part of the city are too narrow for two-way traffic.

5. Jimmy isn't old enough to ride on the bus by himself.
6. Jules had to rewrite his composition because he made too many careless mistakes in grammar and spelling in the first one.
7. There aren't enough seats in the classroom for everyone assigned to this class.
8. We couldn't go to the musical because we waited too long to call the box office for tickets.

◇ **PRACTICE 5, p. 166.**

1. B	5. B
2. A	6. A
3. B	7. B
4. B	

◇ **PRACTICE 6, p. 167.**

1. B	5. A
2. A	6. B
3. B	7. B
4. B	8. A

◇ **PRACTICE 7, p. 167.**

1. B	6. A	11. A
2. D	7. B	12. A
3. A	8. C	13. B
4. C	9. B	14. B
5. B	10. D	15. D

◇ **PRACTICE 8, p. 169.**

1. B	5. B
2. D	6. A
3. D	7. A
4. C	

◇ **PRACTICE 9, p. 169.**

1. to be told
2. having written *(also possible:* writing)
3. being asked/having been asked
4. to have been given
5. being photographed
6. to have had
7. to be sent
8. to be told
9. to have recovered . . . to be
10. having had

◇ **PRACTICE 10, p. 170.**

1. My mother was angry about **my losing** (OR: **having lost**) my new watch.
2. We look forward to **their spending** their vacation with us.
3. No one can understand **Tony's failing** (OR: **having failed**) the economics test even though . . .
4. I am upset about the **students being required** to pay an extra fee to use the laboratory.
5. The supervisor appreciated **Mary's working** (OR: **having worked**) late to finish the project.

◇ PRACTICE 11, p. 170.

1. D	6. D	11. D
2. A	7. B	12. C
3. C	8. C	13. B
4. A	9. D	14. C
5. A	10. B	15. A

◇ PRACTICE 12, p. 172.

1. practice
2. prevent
3. win
4. arrive
5. emerge *(also possible:* emerging*)*
6. perform *(also possible:* performing*)*
7. climb *(also possible:* climbing*)*
8. chirp *(also possible:* chirping*)*
9. explain
10. melt

◇ PRACTICE 13, p. 173.

1. C	6. B
2. A, B	7. A
3. A	8. A, B
4. A	9. A
5. C	10. A

◇ PRACTICE 14, p. 173.

1. B	11. B
2. A	12. A
3. B	13. A
4. C	14. C
5. C	15. D
6. D	16. D
7. D	17. D
8. B	18. B
9. B	19. D
10. C	20. C

◇ PRACTICE 15, p. 175.

1. to buy
2. opening
3. being asked
4. having
5. to wear . . . dressing
6. jumping . . . falling
7. being taken
8. to stop delivering . . . to fill
9. gazing . . . (in order) to cheer
10. having
11. being
12. to move
13. to help . . . resolve/to resolve . . . not to interfere
14. to apply
15. to learn . . . to discover . . . promoting
16. reminding . . . to lock . . . trying to remember
17. asking . . . forgetting
18. not to sign
19. notifying . . . to call
20. play

21. burning . . . coming
22. to be . . . (to) listen
23. thinking
24. tear
25. doing
26. going
27. to be admitted
28. take
29. translate
30. to say . . . understand
31. to begin
32. to be done
33. to discover
34. put
35. feel . . . to be intimidated
36. failing
37. twiddling
38. draw
39. laugh
40. open
41. sleeping
42. to pay
43. being . . . to expect
44. lying

◇ PRACTICE 16, p. 178.

1. to have . . . built . . . to do
2. watch . . . practice . . . finding
3. hearing . . . play . . . forgetting . . . making . . . to relax . . . enjoy
4. wasting . . . to fail . . . doing
5. Attending . . . embarrassing . . . to hide . . . get [parallel infinitives] . . . leave
6. recalling . . . being chosen . . . looking . . . laughing . . . acting . . . playing . . . being . . . achieving
7. cleaning/to be cleaned . . . sweeping/to be swept . . . washing/to be washed . . . dusting/to be dusted . . . Reading . . . doing
8. having been given . . . forming . . . to accept . . . going . . . being . . . having been exposed
9. Finding . . . to be . . . being exposed . . . staying . . . to avoid . . . to minimize . . . getting . . . to get . . . eat [parallel infinitives] . . . taking . . . to prevent catching
10. being inconvenienced or hurt [parallel passive gerunds] . . . to remind . . . to remove . . . to turn . . . to buckle ["buckle up" = connect one's seat belt] . . . to shut . . . to fill . . . to forget to do . . . driving . . . (to) avoid making . . . being instructed . . . to perform . . . being reminded to carry

◇ PRACTICE 17. Test A, p. 181.

1. A	11. B
2. B	12. D
3. D	13. B
4. A	14. B
5. B	15. C
6. D	16. C
7. C	17. D
8. D	18. C
9. D	19. A
10. A	20. B

◇ **PRACTICE 18. Test B, p. 183.**

1.	D	11.	D
2.	D	12.	A
3.	A	13.	C
4.	B	14.	D
5.	B	15.	A
6.	C	16.	C
7.	C	17.	D
8.	C	18.	C
9.	B	19.	A
10.	A	20.	D

Chapter 16: COORDINATING CONJUNCTIONS

◇ **PRACTICE 1, p. 185.**

1. fresh and sweet
2. apples and pears
3. washed and dried
4. am washing and drying
5. happily and quickly
6. biting and tasting
7. to bite and (to) taste
8. delicious but expensive
9. apples, pears, and bananas
10. red, ripe, and juicy

◇ **PRACTICE 2, p. 185.**

1. *(no commas)*
2. Jack was calm, quiet,⋆ and serene.
3. *(no commas)*
4. The children sang, danced,⋆ and played games.
5. *(no commas)*
6. Tom, Tariq,⋆ and Francisco joined in the soccer game.
7. I told the children to sit down, be quiet,⋆ and open their reading books.
8. *(no commas)*
9. *(no commas)*
10. Our waitress's tray held two cups of coffee, three glasses of water,⋆ and one glass of orange juice.
11. *(no commas)*
12. *(no commas) [Answer to question: larger]*

◇ **PRACTICE 3, p. 186.**

1. **I:** for his <u>intelligence</u>, cheerful <u>disposition</u>, and **honesty**
2. **C:** was a <u>lawyer</u> and a <u>politician</u>
3. **I:** <u>smoothly</u> and **quietly**
4. **C:** Barb <u>studies</u> . . . and <u>works</u>
5. **C:** is <u>plentiful</u> and relatively <u>inexpensive</u>
6. **I:** enjoy <u>visiting</u> Disneyland and **touring** movie studios
7. **C:** are usually <u>interested in</u> but a little <u>frightened by</u>
8. **I:** Fainting can result from **either** a <u>lack of oxygen</u> or a <u>loss of blood</u>.
9. **I:** how <u>to write</u> . . . , <u>organize</u> . . . , and **summarize**
10. **C:** not <u>coffee</u> but <u>chocolate</u>
11. **I:** Not only <u>universities</u> but **also many government agencies** support medical research.

⋆ The comma before ***and*** in a series is optional.

12. **C:** explains <u>why water freezes</u> and <u>how the sun produces heat</u>
13. **C:** need <u>light</u>, a suitable <u>climate</u>, and an ample <u>supply</u> *(also possible: of <u>water</u> and <u>minerals</u>)*
14. **C:** With their keen <u>sight</u>, fine <u>hearing</u>, and refined <u>sense of smell</u> *(also possible:* hunt <u>day</u> or <u>night</u>*) (also possible:* of <u>elk</u>, <u>deer</u>, <u>moose</u>, or <u>caribou</u>*)*
15. **I:** by <u>telling</u> jokes and **making** funny faces
16. **C:** is always <u>understanding</u>, <u>patient</u>, and <u>sensitive</u>
17. **C:** Not only the <u>post office</u> but also all <u>banks</u> close
18. **I:** <u>Walking</u> briskly for 30 minutes or **running** for 15 minutes

◇ **PRACTICE 4, p. 187.**

1.	D	5.	F
2.	A	6.	E
3.	B	7.	H
4.	G	8.	C

◇ **PRACTICE 5, p. 187.**

1.	knows	5.	know	9.	agrees
2.	know	6.	wants	10.	are
3.	knows	7.	like	11.	realizes
4.	know	8.	has	12.	think

◇ **PRACTICE 6, p. 188.**

1. Many people drink **neither coffee nor alcohol**.
2. Barbara is fluent in **not only Chinese but also Japanese**. OR: . . . not only in Chinese but also in Japanese.
3. I'm sorry to say that Paul has **neither patience nor sensitivity** to others.
4. She can **both sing and dance**.
5. . . . you should talk to **either your teacher or your academic counselor**. OR: . . . talk either to your teacher or to your academic counselor.
6. Diana is **both intelligent and very creative**.
7. You may begin working **either tomorrow or next week**.
8. Michael told **neither** his **mother nor his father** . . . .
9. . . . requires **not only balance and skill but also concentration and mental alertness**.

◇ **PRACTICE 7, p. 189.**

1. . . . cooking. **My** wife . . . .
2. . . . cooking, *(optional comma)* but my wife . . . .
3. . . . that book. **It's** very good.
4. . . . that book, but I didn't like it.
5. *(Add no punctuation.)*
6. . . . the door. **My** sister answered . . . .
7. . . . the door, *(optional comma)*
8. . . . materials. **They** are found in rocks and soil.
9. . . . are minerals. **They** are found in rocks, soil, and water.
10. . . . by plane, *(optional comma)* or you can go . . . .
11. *(Add no punctuation.)*
12. . . . all night, so he declined . . . .
13. . . . invitation to dinner. **He** needed to . . . .
14. . . . howling outside, yet it was warm . . . .
15. . . . answer the phone, for I didn't want . . . .

16. . . . went camping. It rained the entire time.
17. . . . under construction, so we had to take . . . .
18. . . . win the championship, yet our team won . . . .
19. . . . at the theatre late, but the play had not yet begun. We were quite surprised.
20. . . . from one central place. Most central heating systems service only one building, but some systems heat a group of buildings, such as those at a military base, a campus, or an apartment complex.

◇ PRACTICE 8, p. 189.

I spent yesterday with my brother. We had a really good time. He's visiting me for a couple of days, so I decided not to go to work yesterday. We spent the day in the city. First I took him to the waterfront. We went to the aquarium, where we saw fearsome sharks, some wonderfully funny marine mammals, *(optional comma)* and all kinds of tropical fish. After the aquarium, we went downtown to a big mall and went shopping. My brother doesn't like to shop as much as I do, so we didn't stay there long.

I had trouble thinking of a place to take him for lunch, for he's a strict vegetarian. Luckily I finally remembered a restaurant that has vegan food, so we went there and had a wonderful lunch of fresh vegetables and whole grains. I'm not a vegetarian, yet I must say that I really enjoyed the meal.

In the afternoon, *(optional comma)* it started raining, so we went to a movie. It was pretty good but had too much violence for me. I felt tense when we left the theater. I prefer comedies or dramas. My brother loved the movie.

We ended the day with a good homecooked meal and some good talk in my living room. It was a good day. I like spending time with my brother.

◇ PRACTICE 9, p. 190.

Some of the most interesting working women of the American West in the nineteenth century were African-American women. Mary Fields was one of them. She had been born a slave in the mid-1800s in the South but moved west to the Rocky Mountains as a free woman in 1884. Her first job was hauling freight. She drove a wagon and delivered freight in the valleys and mountains of Montana. She was tall, strong, *(optional comma)* and fast on the draw. She didn't hesitate to protect her wagon of goods with her gun.

She drove a freight wagon for many years. Then in her late fifties, *(optional comma)* she opened a restaurant, but her business failed. In her sixties, *(optional comma)* she became a stagecoach driver carrying the U.S. mail. Because of outlaws, driving a mailcoach was dangerous, yet her mailcoach always arrived safely. In her seventies, *(optional comma)* she opened her own laundry business. She continued successfully in that business until her death in 1914.

Mary Fields deserves our respect and can be seen as a role model for young women, for she rose above unfortunate circumstances and became a determined, hardworking, *(optional comma)* and successful businesswoman.

Chapter 17: ADVERB CLAUSES

◇ PRACTICE 1, p. 191.

1. We'll all take a walk in the park <u>after Dad finishes working on the car</u>.
   <u>After Dad finishes working on the car</u>, we'll all take a walk in the park.
2. <u>Since Douglas fell off his bicycle last week</u>, he has had to use crutches to walk.
   Douglas has had to use crutches to walk <u>since he fell off his bicycle last week</u>.
3. <u>Because I already had my boarding pass</u>, I didn't have to stand in line at the airline counter.
   I didn't have to stand in line at the airline counter <u>because I already had my boarding pass</u>.
4. Productivity in a factory increases <u>if the workplace is made pleasant</u>.
   <u>If the workplace is made pleasant</u>, productivity in a factory increases.
5. <u>After Ceylon had been independent for 24 years</u>, the country's name was changed to Sri Lanka.
   Ceylon's name was changed to Sri Lanka <u>after the country had been independent for 24 years</u>.
6. Ms. Johnson regularly returns her e-mail messages <u>as soon as she has some free time from her principal duties</u>.
   <u>As soon as Ms. Johnson has some free time from her principal duties</u>, she regularly returns her e-mail messages.
7. Tariq will be able to work more efficiently <u>once he becomes familiar with the new computer program</u>.
   <u>Once Tariq becomes familiar with the new computer program</u>, he will be able to work more efficiently.
8. <u>When the flooding river raced down the valley</u>, it destroyed everything in its path.
   The flooding river destroyed everything in its path <u>when it raced down the valley</u>.

◇ PRACTICE 2, p. 191.

1. The lake was calm. Tom went fishing.
2. Because the lake was calm, Tom went fishing.
3. Tom went fishing because the lake was calm. He caught two fish.
4. Tom went fishing because the lake was calm and caught two fish.
5. When Tom went fishing, the lake was calm. He caught two fish.
6. The lake was calm, so Tom went fishing. He caught two fish.
7. Because the lake was calm and quiet, Tom went fishing.
8. The lake was calm, quiet, and clear when Tom went fishing.

9. Mr. Hood is admired because he dedicated his life to helping the poor. **H**e is well known for his work on behalf of homeless people.
10. Microscopes, automobile dashboards, and cameras are awkward for left-handed people to use. **T**hey are designed for right-handed people. **W**hen "lefties" use these items, they have to use their right hand to do the things that they would normally do with their left hand.

◇ **PRACTICE 3, p. 192.**

1. C	5. C	9. C
2. C	6. D	10. A
3. D	7. B	11. D
4. C	8. B	12. A

◇ **PRACTICE 4, p. 193.**

1. My registration was canceled <u>because I didn't pay my fees on time</u>.
   <u>Because I didn't pay my fees on time</u>, my registration was canceled.
2. <u>Now that Erica has qualified for the Olympics in speedskating</u>, she must train even more vigorously. Erica must train even more vigorously <u>now that she has qualified for the Olympics in speedskating</u>.
3. We decided not to buy the house on Fourth Street <u>since it's directly below flight patterns from the nearby international airport</u>.
   <u>Since the house on Fourth Street is directly below flight patterns from the nearby international airport</u>, we decided not to buy it.

◇ **PRACTICE 5, p. 193.**

1. even though
2. because
3. Because
4. Even though
5. Even though
6. Because
7. even though
8. because
9. even though
10. because
11. Even though
12. because
13. Even though . . . because
14. even though . . . because

◇ **PRACTICE 6, p. 194.**

1. C	4. C	7. C
2. C	5. C	8. C
3. C	6. C	9. I

◇ **PRACTICE 7, p. 194.**

1. Let's not go to the park if it ~~will rain~~ rains tomorrow.
2. *(no change)*
3. *(no change)*
4. I'll send you an e-mail if I ~~will have~~ have some free time tomorrow.

5. <u>If we don't leave within the next ten minutes, we</u> ~~are~~ will be late to the theater.
6. <u>If we ~~will leave~~ leave within the next two minutes</u>, we will make it to the theater on time.

◇ **PRACTICE 8, p. 194.**

1. doesn't approve . . . approves
2. can afford . . . can't afford
3. is raining . . . isn't raining
4. don't understand . . . understand

◇ **PRACTICE 9, p. 195.**

1. In case . . . with me, I'll . . . .
2. **W**e'll . . . in case you need to call us.
3. **I**n case you find that you need help with it, she'll be . . . .
4. **M**y boss . . . in case the company . . . .
5. **I**n case I'm not back . . . dinner, I put the . . . .
6. **I**n the event that Janet . . . tomorrow she will . . . .
7. **Y**ou'd better . . . in the event that you run out of cash.
8. **M**y family . . . the country in the event that there is civil war.
9. . . . safe side, I always . . . carry-on bag in the event that the airline loses my luggage.
10. **S**he has already . . . speech in the event that she wins it tonight.

◇ **PRACTICE 10, p. 196.**

1. B
2. A
3. B
4. B
5. A
6. B

◇ **PRACTICE 11, p. 196.**

1. pass
2. not going to go
3. rains
4. only if
5. always eat
6. even if
7. won't
8. don't wake
9. if
10. Don't borrow

◇ **PRACTICE 12, p. 197.**

1. Only if you help me **can I finish** this work on time.
2. If you help me, **I can finish** this work on time.
3. Only if I am invited **will I go**.
4. If I am invited, **I will go**.
5. Only if I am hungry **do I eat**.
6. If I am hungry during the morning, I usually **eat** some fruit.
7. Only if you know both Arabic and Spanish **will you be considered** for that job.

8. Only if the refrigerator is empty **does John go** to the market.
9. Only if you promise not to get angry **will I tell** you the truth about what happened.
10. If you can't learn to communicate your feelings, **I won't marry** you.

◇ **PRACTICE 13, p. 197.**

1. B	5. B	9. C
2. C	6. C	10. C
3. D	7. D	11. D
4. A	8. B	12. A

Chapter 18: REDUCTION OF ADVERB CLAUSES TO MODIFYING ADVERBIAL PHRASES

◇ **PRACTICE 1, p. 199.**

1. Since opening . . . .
2. . . . before leaving the room.
3. While herding his goats . . . .
4. Before marching into battle, ...
5. After meeting/having met the movie star . . . .
6. . . . keys after searching through . . . .
7. When first brought . . . .
8. Since (being) imported into Australia many years ago, the rabbit . . . .

◇ **PRACTICE 2, p. 199.**

1. While <u>Sam</u> was driving to work in the rain, <u>his car</u> got a flat tire.
   → *(no change)*
2. While <u>Sam</u> was driving to work, <u>he</u> had a flat tire.
   → *While driving to work, Sam had a flat tire.*
3. Before <u>Nick</u> left on his trip, <u>his son</u> gave him a big hug and a kiss.
   → *(no change)*
4. Before <u>Nick</u> left on his trip, <u>he</u> gave his itinerary to his secretary.
   → *Before leaving on his trip, Nick gave . . . .*
5. After <u>Tom</u> had worked hard in the garden all afternoon, <u>he</u> took a shower and then went to the movies with his friends.
   → *After having worked hard in the garden all afternoon, Tom took . . . .*
6. After <u>Sunita</u> had made a delicious chicken curry for her friends, <u>they</u> wanted the recipe.
   → *(no change)*
7. Before <u>a friend</u> tries to do something hard, <u>an American</u> may say "Break a leg!" to wish him or her good luck.
   → *(no change)*
8. <u>Emily</u> always straightens her desk before she leaves the office at the end of the day.
   → *Emily always straightens her desk before leaving the office at the end of the day.*

◇ **PRACTICE 3, p. 200.**

1. a. leaving . . . b. left
2. a. invented/had invented . . . b. inventing/having invented
3. a. working . . . b. was working

4. a. flies . . . b. flying
5. a. studied/had studied . . . b. studying/having studied
6. a. learning . . . b. learned
7. a. is taken . . . b. taken
8. a. taking . . . b. take
9. a. was driving . . . b. driving

◇ **PRACTICE 4, p. 201.**

1. Not wanting to disturb his sleeping wife, Larry tiptoed out of the room.
2. *(no change)*
3. Misunderstanding the directions to the hotel, I arrived one hour late for the dinner party.
4. *(no change)*
5. Misunderstanding my directions to the hotel, the taxi driver took me to the wrong place.
6. Remembering that she hadn't turned off the oven, Ann went directly home.
7. *(no change)*
8. Living in the Pacific Northwest, where it rains a great deal, my family and I are accustomed to cool, damp weather.

◇ **PRACTICE 5, p. 201.**

1. E	7. I	
2. J	8. H	
3. A	9. C	
4. G	10. K	
5. B	11. F	
6. L	12. D	

◇ **PRACTICE 6, p. 202.**

1. arriving at the airport
2. reaching the other side of the lake
3. investigating the cause
4. learning the problem was not at all serious
5. being told she got it

◇ **PRACTICE 7, p. 202.**

1. I	6. I	
2. C	7. I	
3. I	8. I	
4. C	9. I	
5. I	10. C	

◇ **PRACTICE 8. Test A, p. 204.**

1. B	11. A	
2. D	12. D	
3. C	13. C	
4. C	14. A	
5. C	15. B	
6. A	16. D	
7. D	17. B	
8. B	18. A	
9. C	19. C	
10. D	20. C	

◇ **PRACTICE 9. Test B, p. 206.**

1. D	11. B
2. B	12. C
3. A	13. B
4. D	14. D
5. C	15. A
6. C	16. D
7. D	17. A
8. B	18. C
9. B	19. D
10. A	20. A

Chapter 19: CONNECTIVES THAT EXPRESS CAUSE AND EFFECT, CONTRAST, AND CONDITION

◇ **PRACTICE 1, p. 208.**
1. because of
2. because
3. because of
4. because
5. because of
6. because
7. because
8. because of

◇ **PRACTICE 2, p. 208.**
1. because
2. Therefore
3. Therefore
4. because
5. Because
6. therefore

◇ **PRACTICE 3, p. 209.**
PART I.
1. Because
2. . . . rained. Therefore, we . . .
3. because of
4. . . . town. Therefore, all . . .
5. because of
6. Because the hurricane . . . town, all . . . .
7. because of
PART II.
8. Due to his poor eyesight, John . . . .
9. Since John has poor eyesight, he . . . .
10. . . . eyesight. Consequently, he . . . .
11. . . . heights. Consequently, she . . . .
12. due to
13. . . . overweight. Consequently, his doctor . . . .
14. Since a diamond . . . hard, it can . . . .

◇ **PRACTICE 4, p. 209.**
1. Edward missed the final exam. **Therefore,** he failed the course. *(also possible: . . . exam; therefore, he failed . . . .)*
2. *(no change)*
3. Edward missed the final exam. **He** simply forgot to go to it. *(also possible: . . . exam; he simply . . . .)*
4. Because we forgot to make a reservation, we couldn't get a table at our favorite restaurant last night.
5. The waitress kept dropping trays full of dishes. **Therefore,** she was fired. *(also possible: . . . dishes; therefore, she was . . . .)*
6. The waiter kept forgetting customers' orders, so he was fired.
7. *(no change)*
8. The needle has been around since prehistoric times. **The** button was invented about 2000 years ago. **The** zipper wasn't invented until 1890.
9. It is possible for wildlife observers to identify individual zebras because the patterns of stripes on each zebra are unique. **No** two zebras are alike. *(also possible: . . . are unique; no two zebras . . . .)*
10. *(no change)*

◇ **PRACTICE 5, p. 210.**
1. such
2. so
3. so
4. such
5. such
6. so
7. so
8. such
9. so
10. so

◇ **PRACTICE 6, p. 210.**
1. It was *such* a nice day *that* we took a walk.
2. The weather was *so* hot *that* you could fry an egg on the sidewalk.
3. She talked *so* fast *that* I couldn't understand her.
4. It was *such* an expensive car *that* we couldn't afford to buy it.
5. We're having *such* beautiful weather *that* I don't feel like going to class.
6. Grandpa held me *so* tightly when he hugged me *that* I couldn't breathe for a moment.
7. There were *so* few people at the meeting *that* it was canceled.
8. The classroom has *such* comfortable chairs *that* the students find it easy to fall asleep.
9. Ted was *so* worried about the exam *that* he couldn't get to sleep last night.
10. Jerry got *so* angry *that* he put his fist through the wall.
11. I have *so* many problems *that* I can use all the help you can give me.
12. The tornado struck with *such* great force *that* it lifted automobiles off the ground.
13. His handwriting is *so* illegible *that* I can't figure out what this sentence says.
14. David has *so* many girlfriends *that* he can't remember all of their names.
15. *So* many people came to the meeting *that* there were not enough seats for everyone.

◇ **PRACTICE 7, p. 211.**
1. Rachel turned on the TV *so that she could watch* the news.
2. Alex wrote down the time and date of his appointment *so that he wouldn't forget* to go.
3. Nancy is carrying extra courses every semester *so that she can graduate* early.

4. Jason is tired of work and school and is planning to take a semester off *so that he can travel in* Europe.
5. Suzanne lowered the volume on the TV set *so that she wouldn't disturb* her roommate.
6. Whenever we are planning a vacation, we call a travel agent *so that we can get* expert advice on our itinerary.
7. It's a good idea for you to learn how to type *so that you can type* your own papers when you go to the university.
8. Lynn tied a string around her finger so that *she wouldn't forget* to take her book back to the library.
9. Ed took some change from his pocket *so that he could buy* a newspaper.
10. I turned on the TV *so that I could listen* to the news while I was making dinner.
11. I unplugged the phone *so that I wouldn't be interrupted* while I was working.
12. Yesterday Linda was driving on the highway when her car started making strange noises. After she pulled over to the side of the road, she raised the hood of her car *so that other drivers would know* that she had car trouble.

◇ **PRACTICE 8, p. 212.**

1. D	6. C	11. A
2. A	7. A	12. B
3. C	8. C	13. B
4. D	9. B	14. C
5. D	10. C	15. D

◇ **PRACTICE 9, p. 213.**
1. Annie told the truth, but no one believed her.
2. Annie told the truth. **H**owever, no one believed her. *(also possible:* . . . the truth; however, no one . . . .*)*
3. Even though Annie told the truth, no one believed her.
4. *(no change)*
5. Annie told the truth, yet no one believed her.
6. Annie told the truth. **N**evertheless, no one believed her. *(also possible:* . . . the truth; nevertheless, no one . . . .*)*
7. In spite of the fact that Annie told the truth, no one believed her.
8. *(no change)*
9. Even though all of my family friends have advised me not to travel abroad during this time of political turmoil, I'm leaving next week to begin a trip around the world.
10. Some people think great strides have been made in cleaning up the environment in much of the world. **H**owever, others think the situation is much worse than it was twenty years ago. *(also possible:* of the world; however, others think . . . .*)*

◇ **PRACTICE 10, p. 213.**
1. a. Even though
   b. Despite
   c. Despite
   d. Despite
   e. Even though

2. a. In spite of
   b. Although
   c. Although
   d. In spite of
   e. In spite of
3. a. Despite
   b. Although
   c. Despite
   d. Although
   e. Despite
4. a. In spite of
   b. Even though
   c. in spite of
   d. even though
   e. in spite of
   f. even though
   g. even though
   h. in spite of

◇ **PRACTICE 11, p. 215.**

1. B	6. H
2. E	7. A
3. J	8. G
4. F	9. I
5. C	10. D

◇ **PRACTICE 12, p. 216.**
1. Red is bright and lively, *while* gray is a dull color.
   OR
   While red is bright and lively, gray is a dull color.

2. Jane is insecure and unsure of herself. Her sister, *on the other hand*, is full of self-confidence. *(also possible:* . . . of herself; her sister, *on the other hand*, is . . . .*)*
   OR
   Jane is insecure and unsure of herself. *On the other hand*, her sister is full of self-confidence. OR
   Jane is insecure and unsure of herself. Her sister is full of self-confidence, *on the other hand*.

3. A rock is heavy, *while* a feather is light. OR
   While a rock is heavy, a feather is light.

4. Some children are unruly, *whereas* others are quiet and obedient. OR
   Whereas some children are unruly, others are quiet and obedient.

5. Language and literature classes are easy and enjoyable for Alex. Math and science courses, *on the other hand*, are difficult for him. *(also possible:* . . . for Alex; math and science courses, *on the other hand*, are difficult . . . .*)* OR
   Language and literature classes are easy and enjoyable for Alex. *On the other hand*, math and science courses are difficult for him. OR
   Language and literature classes are easy and enjoyable for Alex. Math and science courses are difficult for him, *on the other hand*.

6. Strikes can bring improvements in wages and working conditions. *However*, strikes can also cause loss of jobs and bankruptcy. *(also possible:* . . . conditions; *however*, strikes can . . . .*)* OR
   Strikes can bring improvements in wages and working conditions. Strikes can also, *however*,

cause loss of jobs and bankruptcy. OR
Strikes can bring improvements in wages and
working conditions. Strikes can also cause loss of
jobs and bankruptcy, *however*. OR
Strikes can bring improvements in wages and
working conditions. Strikes can also, *however*, cause
loss of jobs and bankruptcy.

◇ **PRACTICE 13, p. 216.**

1. even though/although
2. due to/because of
3. even though/although
4. Nevertheless/However
5. Even though/Although
6. In spite of/Despite
7. Therefore
8. on the other hand/however
9. because of/due to
10. Although/Even though
11. because/since
12. Even though/Although
13. because of/due to
14. Therefore
15. Although/Even though (*also possible:* While)
16. Because/Since

◇ **PRACTICE 14, p. 217.**

1. You should (had better/have to/must) eat less and get more exercise. Otherwise, you won't lose weight.
2. The children have to (had better/should/ must) finish all of their chores. Otherwise, they cannot watch TV tonight.
3. You have to (must/should/had better) speak up now. Otherwise, the boss will go ahead . . . .
4. You must (had better/should/have to) stop at the store on your way home from work. Otherwise, we won't have anything . . . .
5. You had better (have to/should/must) think it through very carefully. Otherwise, you won't come up . . . .
6. We have to (had better/should/must) catch fish this morning. Otherwise, we're going to have beans for dinner again.
7. You should (had better/have to/must) get someone to help you. Otherwise, it's going to be very . . . .
8. Maria had better (should/has to/must) find a way to convince the boss that the error was unavoidable. Otherwise, she'll probably lose her job.

◇ **PRACTICE 15, p. 218.**

1. passes
2. doesn't pass
3. passes
4. passes
5. doesn't pass
6. passes
7. doesn't pass
8. doesn't pass
9. must/has to pass
10. had better (must/has to) pass

◇ **PRACTICE 16. Test A, p. 219.**

1. C	14. A
2. A	15. C
3. C	16. B
4. C	17. A
5. A	18. A
6. C	19. B
7. C	20. B
8. B	21. B
9. D	22. B
10. A	23. D
11. B	24. A
12. C	25. C
13. B	

◇ **PRACTICE 17. Test B, p. 221.**

1. B	14. A
2. A	15. A
3. D	16. B
4. B	17. D
5. C	18. C
6. D	19. A
7. C	20. B
8. C	21. A
9. C	22. D
10. B	23. A
11. C	24. A
12. B	25. A
13. B	

**Chapter 20: CONDITIONAL SENTENCES
AND WISHES**

◇ **PRACTICE 1, p. 223.**

1. were . . . would take
2. would accept . . . were
3. will explode/explodes . . . throw
4. were . . . would call . . . (would) talk
5. is . . . will be canceled
6. consisted . . . would be

◇ **PRACTICE 2, p. 223.**

1. had told . . . would have given
2. wouldn't have gotten/got . . . had remembered
3. had known . . . wouldn't have voted
4. would have gotten/got . . . had used
5. had written . . . wouldn't have lost
6. would you have taken . . . had known

◇ **PRACTICE 3, p. 224.**

1. had . . . wouldn't have to
2. Would people be . . . had
3. send . . . will arrive
4. had brought . . . wouldn't have had
5. felt . . . would drop
6. have . . . will always rise . . . flood OR: always rises . . . floods
7. discover . . . will call
8. had known . . . would have stayed up . . . (would have) finished

PRACTICE 4, p. 225.

1. If I hadn't been sick yesterday, I would have gone to class.
2. If Alan ate breakfast, he wouldn't overeat at lunch.
3. Kostas wouldn't have been late to his own wedding if his watch hadn't been slow.
4. I would ride the bus to work every morning if it weren't always so crowded.
5. If Sara had known that highway 57 was closed, she would have taken an alternative route.
6. Camille could have finished unloading the truck if someone had been there to help her.

PRACTICE 5, p. 225.

1. weren't raining . . . would finish
2. had eaten . . . wouldn't be
3. hadn't left . . . would have
4. would have answered . . . hadn't been studying
5. hadn't been shining . . . wouldn't have gone
6. wouldn't ache . . . hadn't played
7. wouldn't stop . . . weren't running
8. had eaten . . . wouldn't have to have
9. hadn't been playing . . . would have heard
10. weren't closing . . . wouldn't have to leave

PRACTICE 6, p. 226.

1. If the wind **weren't blowing** hard, I **would take** the boat out for a ride.
2. I **wouldn't feel** better now if you **hadn't talked** to me about my problems last night.
3. If Ann **hadn't carried** heavy furniture when she helped her friend move, her back **wouldn't hurt** now.
4. If Paulo **weren't working** on two jobs right now, he **would have time** to help you with your remodeling.
5. If I **had been working** at the restaurant last night, I **would have waited** on your table.
6. If Diane **hadn't asked questions** every time she didn't understand a problem, she **wouldn't have** a good understanding of geometry now.
7. If a fallen tree **hadn't been blocking** the road, we **would have arrived** on time.
8. Rita **wouldn't be** exhausted today if she **had gotten** some sleep last night.
9. If Olga and Ivan **had been paying** attention, they **would have seen** the sign marking their exit from the highway.
10. If the doctor really **cared** about his patients, he **would have explained** the medical procedure to me before surgery.

PRACTICE 7, p. 227.

1. Should you need
2. Were I you
3. Had I been offered
4. Should anyone call
5. Were I
6. had they known
7. were she
8. Had I not opened

PRACTICE 8, p. 227.

1. Were I your age, I'd do things differently.
2. Should Bob show up while I'm away, please give him my message.

3. Had my uncle stood up to sing, I'd have been embarrassed.
4. Were she ever in trouble, I'd do anything I could to help her.
5. Should the manager question these figures, have her talk to the bookkeeper.
6. I wouldn't have known about your new job had I not talked to your mother. [*Had* and *not* are not contracted in the omitted-*if* pattern.]

PRACTICE 9, p. 227.

1. . . . I hadn't forgotten to tell him that she needed a ride.
2. . . . I hadn't had your help.
3. If I hadn't opened the door slowly . . . .
4. . . . he could have gotten/got time off from work.
5. . . . he had told his boss about the problem.

PRACTICE 10, p. 228.

1. D	11. C
2. B	12. A
3. D	13. B
4. D	14. D
5. C	15. C
6. A	16. B
7. C	17. B
8. B	18. B
9. C	19. A
10. D	20. C

PRACTICE 11, p. 229.

1. would have . . . hadn't spent
2. would have been hit . . . hadn't pulled
3. would have been (*also possible:* could have been)
4. would think
5. would have done (*also possible:* could have done)
6. wouldn't say . . . meant
7. would have graduated (*also possible:* could have graduated)
8. had been driving fast . . . would have been
9. travels . . . always spends

PRACTICE 12, p. 230.

1. were
2. had been made
3. had . . . met
4. were
5. hadn't heard
6. didn't have/hadn't
7. didn't exist
8. had happened
9. were
10. were
11. had stopped
12. had appeared

PRACTICE 13, p. 231.

1. were shining
2. had gone
3. had driven
4. could swim
5. would stop

6. had won
7. had gotten
8. hadn't quit
9. were
10. would sing
11. could bring
12. had offered

◇ PRACTICE 14, p. 232.

1. had not missed
2. A: would stop   B: were shining
3. had gone . . . could paint
4. hadn't moved . . . had taken
5. would stop
6. hadn't paid
7. A: would hurry   B: would relax
8. hadn't invited
9. B: hadn't been elected   A: hadn't voted
10. A: could buy   B: grew
11. A: weren't . . . were   B: were . . . were
12. A: would meet   B: disagreed . . . could prove
13. had told
14. would go

◇ PRACTICE 15, p. 233.

1. had been run
2. would look
3. had had
4. hadn't been driving
5. wouldn't have slid
6. step ["step on the gas" = accelerate the car]
7. hadn't taken
8. wouldn't have lost
9. hadn't lost
10. would have had
11. had had
12. wouldn't have to pay
13. hadn't been driving
14. wouldn't have run into
15. wouldn't be
16. were/was
17. would take
18. stay
19. would stay
20. weren't/wasn't
21. could go
22. I'll fly
23. I'll take
24. could drive
25. would be

◇ PRACTICE 16. Test A, p. 235.

1. B	11. C
2. C	12. B
3. C	13. B
4. A	14. B
5. C	15. D
6. B	16. C
7. D	17. D
8. B	18. B
9. D	19. D
10. A	20. A

◇ PRACTICE 17. Test B, p. 237.

1. D	11. D
2. D	12. B
3. A	13. D
4. C	14. C
5. B	15. B
6. A	16. A
7. D	17. B
8. B	18. D
9. A	19. C
10. C	20. A

Appendix: SUPPLEMENTARY GRAMMAR UNITS

◇ PRACTICE 1, p. A1.

1. Airplanes have wings.
   s   v   o

2. The teacher explained the problem.
       s   v   o

3. Children enjoy games.
   s   v   o

4. Jack wore a blue suit.
   s v   o

5. Some animals eat plants. Some animals eat
       s   v   o   s   v
   other animals.
   o

6. According to an experienced waitress, you
                                   s
   can carry full cups of coffee without spilling
   v   o
   them just by never looking at them.

◇ PRACTICE 2, p. A1.

1. Alice arrived at six o'clock.
       vi

2. We drank some tea.
     vt

3. I agree with you.
     vi

4. I waited for Sam at the airport for two hours.
     vi

5. They're staying at a resort hotel in San Antonio, Texas.
       vi

6. Chanchai is studying English.
       vt

7. The wind is blowing hard today.
       vi

8. I walked to the theater, but Janice rode her bicycle.
     vi   vt

9. Amphibians hatch from eggs.
       vi

10. Rivers flow toward the sea.
      vi

◇ PRACTICE 3, p. A2.

1. Jim came to class <u>without</u> his books.
2. We stayed <u>at</u> home <u>during</u> the storm.
3. Sonya walked <u>across</u> the bridge <u>over</u> the Cedar River.
4. When Alex walked <u>through</u> the door, his little sister ran <u>toward</u> him and put her arms <u>around</u> his neck.
5. The two <u>of</u> us need to talk <u>to</u> Tom, too.
6. Animals live <u>in</u> all parts <u>of</u> the world. Animals walk or crawl <u>on</u> land, fly <u>in</u> the air, and swim <u>in</u> the water.
7. Scientists divide living things <u>into</u> two main groups: the animal kingdom and the plant kingdom.
8. Asia extends <u>from</u> the Pacific Ocean <u>in</u> the east <u>to</u> Africa and Europe <u>in</u> the west.

◇ PRACTICE 4, p. A2.

1.　　 S　　 V　　　 O　　　　 PP
   <u>Jack</u> <u>put</u> the <u>letter</u> <u>in the mailbox</u>.

2.　　　　 S　　　 V　　 PP
   The <u>children</u> <u>walked</u> <u>to school</u>.

3.　　 S　　 V　　　 O　　　　 PP
   <u>Mary</u> <u>did</u> her <u>homework</u> <u>at the library</u>.

4.　　　　　　 S　　　 V
   Chinese <u>printers</u> <u>created</u> the first paper

   　 O　　　 PP
   <u>money</u> <u>in the world</u>.

5.　　　 S　　　 V　　　　 PP
   Dark <u>clouds</u> <u>appeared</u> <u>on the horizon</u>.

6.　　 S　　 V　　　 O　　　　 PP
   <u>Mary</u> <u>filled</u> the <u>shelves</u> <u>of the cabinet</u>

   　　 PP　　　 PP
   <u>with boxes</u> <u>of old books</u>.

◇ PRACTICE 5, p. A2.

1.　　　　　　　 ADJ　　　 ADV
   Jack opened the <u>heavy</u> door <u>slowly</u>.

2.　 ADJ　　　　　　　 ADJ
   <u>Chinese</u> jewelers carved <u>beautiful</u>
   ornaments from jade.

3.　　 ADJ　　　　 ADJ　　　　 ADV
   The <u>old</u> man carves <u>wooden</u> figures <u>skillfully</u>.

4.　　 ADJ　　　　 ADV　　　 ADJ
   A <u>busy</u> executive <u>usually</u> has <u>short</u>
   conversations on the telephone.

5.　　 ADJ　　　　　　 ADV ADJ
   The <u>young</u> woman had a <u>very</u> <u>good</u> time at
   　　　　　 ADV
   the picnic <u>yesterday</u>.

◇ PRACTICE 6, p. A3.

1. quickly
2. quick
3. polite
4. politely
5. regularly
6. regular
7. usual
8. usually
9. well
10. good
11. gentle
12. gently
13. annually
14. annual
15. bad
16. badly

◇ PRACTICE 7, p. A3.

1. Sue **always takes** a walk in the morning.
2. Tim **is always** a hard worker.
3. Beth **has always worked** hard.
4. Jack **always works** hard.
5. **Do you always work** hard?
6. Taxis **are usually** available . . . .
7. Youssef **rarely takes** a taxi . . . .
8. I **have often thought** about . . . .
9. Yuko **probably needs** some help.
10. **Have you ever attended** the show . . . ?
11. Al **seldom goes** out . . . .
12. The students **are hardly ever** late.
13. **Do you usually finish** your . . . ?
14. In India, the monsoon season **generally begins** in April.
15. . . . Mr. Singh's hometown **usually receives** around . . . .

◇ PRACTICE 8, p. A4.

	L.VERB	+ ADJ
1.	Ø (no linking verb in the sentence)	
2.	looked	fresh
3.	Ø	
4.	Ø	
5.	tasted	good
6.	grew	quiet
7.	Ø	
8.	Ø	
9.	Ø	
10.	smells	delicious
11.	Ø	
12.	got	sleepy
13.	became	rough
14.	Ø	
15.	Ø	
16.	sounded	happy
17.	turns	hot
18.	Ø	
19.	Ø	
20.	appears	certain
21.	seems	strange

◇ PRACTICE 9, p. A5.

1. clean
2. slowly
3. safely
4. anxious
5. complete
6. wildly
7. honest
8. thoughtfully
9. well
10. fair
11. terrible
12. good
13. light
14. confidently
15. famous
16. fine

◇ PRACTICE 10, p. A6.

	Question word	Auxiliary verb	Subject	Main verb	Rest of question
1a.	Ø	Can	Bob	live	there?
1b.	Where	can	Bob	live	Ø?
1c.	Who	can	Ø	live	there?
2a.	Ø	Is	Don	living	there?
2b.	Where	is	Don	living	Ø?
2c.	Who	is	Ø	living	there?
3a.	Ø	Does	Sue	live	there?
3b.	Where	does	Sue	live	Ø?
3c.	Who	Ø	Ø	lives	there?
4a.	Ø	Will	Ann	live	there?
4b.	Where	will	Ann	live	Ø?
4c.	Who	will	Ø	live	there?
5a.	Ø	Did	Jack	live	there?
5b.	Where	did	Jack	live	Ø?
5c.	Who	Ø	Ø	lived	there?
6a.	Ø	Has	Mary	lived	there?
6b.	Where	has	Mary	lived	Ø?
6c.	Who	has	Ø	lived	there?

◇ PRACTICE 11, p. A7.

1. When are you going to the zoo?
2. Are you going downtown later today?
3. Do you live in an apartment?
4. Where does Sue live?
5. Who lives in that house?
6. Can you speak French?
7. Who can speak Arabic?
8. When did Olga arrive?
9. Who arrived late?
10. What is Ann opening?
11. What is Ann doing?
12. What did Mary open?
13. Who opened the door?
14. Has the mail arrived?
15. Do you have a bicycle?
16. What does Alex have in his hand?
17. Do you like ice cream?
18. Would you like an ice cream cone?
19. What would Joe like?
20. Who would like a soft drink?

◇ PRACTICE 12, p. A8.

1. How long has Pierre been living here?
2. Which (city) is farther north, London or Paris?
3. Whose is it?
4. What have you been doing?
5. Who answered the phone?
6. How do they plow their fields?
7. How long have you had it?
8. What kind of bird is that?
9. Why were you late for work this morning? (OR: How come you were late for work this morning?)

10. How long did it take you?
11. What time/When did he finally get home?
12. How do you take it?
13. What is the population of the United States?
14. Which (coat/one) do you like better (, the red one or the black one)?
15. How did you get there?
16. Who(m) should I address it to? *(formal:* To whom should I address it?)
17. How far (How many miles) is it from here to Los Angeles?
18. Who is going to be at the meeting tonight?
19. How often (How many times a week) do people in your country have rice?
20. Where did you get that silly looking hat?
21. What does "apologize" mean?
22. How many edges are there on a cube? . . . . How many edges are there on a pyramid?
23. What does he look like?
24. What is she like?

◇ PRACTICE 13, p. A10.

1. How do you take your coffee?
2. What kind of dictionary do you have? (have you?/have you got?)
3. What does he do for a living?
4. Who was Margaret talking to?/To whom was Margaret talking?
5. How many people showed up for the meeting?
6. Why could none of the planes take off?
7. What was she thinking about?/About what was she thinking?
8. How fast/How many miles per hour (OR: an hour) were you driving when the policeman stopped you?
9. What kind of food do you like best?
10. Which apartment is yours/Where is your apartment?
11. What is Oscar like? *(also possible:* What kind of person/man is Oscar?)
12. What does Oscar look like?
13. Whose dictionary fell to the floor?
14. Why isn't Abby here?
15. When will all of the students in the class be informed of their final grades?
16. How do you feel?
17. Which book did you prefer?
18. What kind of music do you like?
19. How late is the plane expected to be?
20. Why did the driver of the stalled car light a flare?
21. Which pen do you want?
22. What's the weather like in July?
23. How do you like your steak?
24. How did you do on the test?
25. How many seconds are there in a year?

◇ PRACTICE 14, p. A11.

1. How much money do you need?
2. Where was Roberto born?/In what country/city was . . .? /What country/city was Roberto born in?
3. How often do you go out to eat?
4. Who(m) are you waiting for? *(very formal and seldom used:* For whom are you waiting?)
5. Who answered the phone?

6. Who(m) did you call?
7. Who called?
8. How much gas/How many gallons of gas did she buy?
9. What does "deceitful" mean?
10. What is an abyss?
11. Which way did he go?
12. Whose books and papers are these?
13. How many children do they have? [British or regional American: How many children have they?]
14. How long has he been here?
15. How far is it/How many miles is it to New Orleans? ["New Orleans" has at least two commonly used pronunciations. Whatever pronunciation your students are familiar with is correct.]
16. When/At what time can the doctor see me?
17. Who **is** her roommate?
18. Who **are** her roommates?
19. How long/How many years have your parents been living there?
20. Whose book is this?
21. Who**'s** coming over for dinner?
22. What color **is** Ann's dress?
23. What color **are** Ann's eyes?
24. Who can't go . . . ?
25. Why **can't Bob** go?/How come **Bob can't** go?
26. Why **didn't you**/How come **you didn't** answer . . . ? (formal and rare: Why **did you not** answer the phone?)
27. What kind of music do you like?
28. What don't you understand?
29. What **is** Janet **doing** right now?
30. How do you spell "sitting"? [you = impersonal pronoun]
31. What **does** Tom **look like**?
32. What **is** Tom **like**?
33. What does Ron do (for a living)?
34. How far/How many miles is Mexico from here?
35. How do you take/like your coffee?
36. Which (city) is farther north, Stockholm or Moscow?/Of Stockholm and Moscow, which (city/one) is farther north?
37. How are you getting along?

◇ **PRACTICE 15, p. A12.**
1. Haven't you seen . . . ? No.
2. Don't you feel . . . ? No.
3. Wasn't he . . . ? No.
4. Didn't Mary tell . . . ? No.
5. Don't Janet and you work . . . ? Yes.
6. Isn't that . . . ? Yes.
7. Wasn't she . . . ? No.
8. Isn't she . . . ? Yes.

◇ **PRACTICE 16, p. A13.**
1. don't you
2. have you
3. didn't she
4. aren't there
5. have you
6. don't you (also possible but less common: haven't you)
7. won't you
8. doesn't he

9. shouldn't we
10. can they
11. are they
12. isn't it
13. did they
14. aren't I/am I not
15. isn't it

◇ **PRACTICE 17, p. A13.**
1. He's
2. Ø
3. He's
4. Ø
5. She'd
6. Ø
7. She'd
8. Ø
9. We'll
10. They're
11. It's
12. It's
13. Ø
14. Ø
15. We're
16. Ø
17. She's
18. She'd
19. She'd . . . we'd
20. Ø . . . he'd

◇ **PRACTICE 18, p. A14.**
1. I don't have any problems. I have no problems.
2. There wasn't any food on the shelf. There was no food on the shelf.
3. I didn't receive any letters from home. I received no letters from home.
4. I don't need any help. I need no help.
5. We don't have any time to waste. We have no time to waste.
6. You shouldn't have given the beggar any money. You should have given the beggar no money.
7. I don't trust anyone. I trust no one/no-one.
8. I didn't see anyone. I saw no one/no-one.
9. There wasn't anyone in his room. There was no one/no-one in his room.
10. She can't find anybody who knows about it. She can find nobody who knows about it.

◇ **PRACTICE 19, p. A15.**
1. We **have no** time to waste. OR: We **don't have any** time to waste.
2. I **didn't have any** problems. OR: I **had no** problems.
3. I **can't do anything** about it. OR: I **can do nothing** about it.
4. You **can hardly ever understand her** when she speaks.
5. I **know neither** Ann **nor** her husband. OR: I **don't know either** Ann **or** her husband.
6. **Don't ever drink** water from . . . . OR: **Never drink** water from . . . .
7. . . . I **could barely hear** the speaker.

◇ **PRACTICE 20, p. A15.**
1. **Hardly had I stepped** out of bed . . . .
2. **Never will I say** that again.
3. **Scarcely ever have I enjoyed** myself more . . . .
4. **Rarely does she make** a mistake.
5. **Never will I trust** him again because . . . .
6. **Hardly ever is it** possible to get . . . .
7. **Seldom do I skip** breakfast.
8. **Never have I known** a more . . . .

◇ **PRACTICE 21, p. A15.**

1. for	6. to	11. to
2. about	7. of	12. of
3. of	8. to	13. for
4. with	9. for	14. of
5. from	10. to	15. with

◇ **PRACTICE 22, p. A16.**

1. in	9. to . . . for
2. for	10. about
3. in	11. from
4. from	12. of
5. to	13. with
6. for	14. with . . . about
7. with	15. to
8. to . . . to	

◇ **PRACTICE 23, p. A16.**

1. of	6. of	11. from
2. of	7. to	12. in
3. of	8. for	13. with
4. for	9. (up)on	14. with
5. to	10. from	15. in

◇ **PRACTICE 24, p. A17.**

1. of	6. with	11. from
2. to	7. to	12. in
3. with	8. for	13. about
4. with	9. to	14. to
5. in	10. from	15. from

◇ **PRACTICE 25, p. A18.**

1. for	7. with	12. from
2. at	8. (up)on . . .	13. with . . .
3. for	(up)on	about
4. to	9. for	14. with
5. in	10. about	15. from
6. of	11. with	

◇ **PRACTICE 26, p. A19.**

1. from	6. with	11. of
2. of	7. for	12. from
3. to	8. for	13. to
4. with	9. in . . . at	14. with
5. to . . . for	10. to	15. with . . . of

Special Workbook Section: PHRASAL VERBS

◇ **PRACTICE 1, p. A22.**
1. up
2. away/out
3. out/off
4. up
5. off [A "raincheck" is a ticket that admits you to the theater another time without additional payment.]
6. up
7. out [from a library; "I.D." is an abbreviation for identification card.]
8. about
9. up
10. back . . . out of

◇ **PRACTICE 2, p. A23.**
1. in
2. on . . . off
3. back
4. in/by (also possible: over)
5. out
6. out
7. up
8. up . . . away/out
9. out . . . back [Note: One "fills out" a large item such as an application form, but "fills in" a small space such as a blank in an exercise. Also: "fill up" (British) = "fill in" (American.]
10. up ["catch up with him" (American) = "catch him up" (British)]
11. on
12. out

◇ **PRACTICE 3, p. A24.**

1. up	6. out
2. in . . . over	7. up
3. up	8. down
4. after/for	9. up
5. up	10. out

◇ **PRACTICE 4, p. A25.**

1. out/around	6. in
2. in/into . . .	7. off
out	8. up
3 along	9. out
4. off	10. over
5. after	

◇ **PRACTICE 5, p. A25.**
1. through [= finish a task]
2. up
3. out ["got dizzy" = had a whirling sensation in the head; *revive* = return to normal breathing; "out cold" = unconscious, in a faint]
4. over ["passed out" = fainted, became suddenly unconscious]

5. up
6. out [= make a line through it with pen or pencil]
7. back
8. on
9. on . . . off
10. into . . . out
11. on . . . off
12. on . . . off

◇ PRACTICE 6, p. A26.

1. on/up
2. over . . . in . . . over
3. up
4. up
5. away/on
6. on
7. over
8. out
9. out of
10. off . . . in
11. up
12. about . . . along with

◇ PRACTICE 7, p. A27

1. into
2. off
3. on
4. back [They are talking on the telephone.]
5. out
6. out . . . across/upon
7. up
8. into . . . out
9. up
10. on/off/out

◇ PRACTICE 8, p. A29.

1. after
2. out
3. up . . . out
4. up [= get ill or sick]
5. up
6. in [= into his office for an appointment]
7. out/into
8. down
9. out ["crash a party" = come without being invited, an impolite act]
10. away